MAKE MONEY ON THE INTERNET

HOW TO TURN YOUR WEBSITE INTO A
CASH MAKING MACHINE

RYAN CHIN
ANGIE SALISBURY

THINK STRATEGY INC.
SEATTLE, WA

Copyright © 2014 by Think Strategy Inc.

All rights reserved. No part of this publication may be reproduced, distributed or transmitted in any form or by any means, including photocopying, recording, or other electronic or mechanical methods, without the prior written permission of the publisher, except in the case of brief quotations embodied in critical reviews and certain other noncommercial uses permitted by copyright law. For permission requests, write to the publisher, addressed "Attention: Permissions Coordinator," at the address below.

Think Strategy Inc.
6727 Seward Park Ave. S.
Seattle, WA 98118
www.thinkstrategy.com

Ordering Information:
Quantity sales. Special discounts are available on quantity purchases by corporations, associations, and others. For details, contact the "Special Sales Department" at the address above.

Make Money on the Internet. —1st ed.
ISBN 978-1502916716

Contents

Beauty Is Only Code Deep	7
Do You Trust Me?	29
The Purpose Driven Page	49
Using Landing Pages for Lead Generation	81
Content is King	101
Where to Get Ideas	102
What To Talk About	114
Setting Up Your Technical Infrastructure for SEO	123
Keyword Research	145
On Page SEO	167
Getting Found in Local Search	177
Social Media Rules of Engagement	193
How to Get Sales with Facebook	211
Become a Digital Pied Piper on Twitter	233
Link In to Business to Business (B2B) Leads	253
Generate Demand with Pictures on Instagram & Pinterest	271

Driving Sales with Search Engine Marketing	289
Build a Virtual Sales Force	307
The After Party	317
What's Next? Start Selling!	327

Thanks to my husband and family for always believing in me and to my two German Shorthaired Pointers for being the greatest sounding boards ever. Look out, it's your turn next.
~ Angie

Dedicated to my family who taught me the importance of helping others.
~ Ryan

Part One

What Differentiates Sites That Sell Well From Ones That Don't?

[1]

Beauty Is Only Code Deep

Beautiful websites can earn you and your company appreciation and recognition from visitors.

Unfortunately, admiration doesn't necessarily lead to sales.

Don't get us wrong, we'd rather have a great looking website than an ugly one. It's just that the beauty is negligible if you're more focused on style and aesthetics but don't think about usability.

Are you too focused on creating a piece of art rather than a functional tool that sells? Do you want people to be impressed with your taste level or do you want them to buy from you?

It's kind of like when you're trying to sell a house and you spend all your money on things that look good to you rather than focusing on what may have the most appeal to the widest pool of buyers. It can be a very costly experience and in the end, you're left sitting in a nice house that you're trying to get rid of.

We're going to help you avoid making the same mistake with your website.

But before we get into the specifics, you have to be sure you understand who you're targeting with your website, and the best way to do that is to create a customer persona.

Creating a Customer Persona

Anytime you're creating content for your site (website copy, articles, images, graphics, videos, pages, etc.), you always need to keep your customer in mind. This is imperative because it takes the focus off of you and puts it onto the people you're trying to reach.

To help you keep focused on the customer, start by creating a persona for them.

A persona is a detailed representation of your average target customer. You may have heard the term "avatar" (not the movie!), and it's basically the same thing. You're imaging who your ideal, perfect customer is.

While most businesses have an idea of their target customer, they tend to think of them on a high level – job title, gender and income. However, if you really want to relate to your target market, you need to be able to define them much more in depth – and that's where a persona comes into play.

Create a persona that represents the majority of your target market and think about them as you develop your site. After you define the first persona, you may decide to create one or two more, but don't do any more than that or the personas become a lot less useful – you start getting too broad rather than targeted.

To come up with a persona, take information on your current customer base and define common elements among them. You can also do research by conducting interviews with people in your target market and through online surveys. Interviews are nice because you can ask people follow-up questions if they say something that surprised you or that you didn't think about earlier.

Online surveys can be less time consuming than doing in-person interviews and can be done using free software such as Survey Monkey, although you won't be able to follow-up with additional questions unless you require the person to provide their contact information (which, unfortunately, may reduce the likelihood of them completing the questionnaire).

Here are some things to consider when defining your persona:

- Name
- Employer
- Job title
- What their company does
- Company size
- Demographics
- Age
- Gender
    - Income
    - Education
    - Family (i.e. marital status, kids, pets)
    - Where they live
- Behaviors
    - Who influences their buying decision (i.e. significant others, kids, coworkers, social media, friends)?
    - How do they spend money?
    - How do they make buying decisions?
    - How tech savvy are they?
    - What motivates them?
- What are they looking for?
    - What are their pain points?
    - What goals/visions do they have?
- What are their favorite websites?
    - News
    - Blogs
    - Entertainment

        o   Shopping
        o   Leisure-related
    •   Hobbies

Persona: "Gus"

Liberato, Ricardo. "Riga Old Man." 26 July 2006. Online image. Flickr. 27 May 2014.
https://www.flickr.com/photos/liberato/200858281

- Retired (previously a sales rep. for a 50,000+ employee pharmaceutical company).

- Male, 72 years old.

- $60,000/year household income.

- Bachelor's Degree in Business.

- Married with two children and four grandchildren.

- Lives in San Diego suburbs.

- Spends his money conservatively on most things, but spends more on leisurely activities (like vacations and hobbies) and family activities. His wife and friends influence his buying decisions. He's motivated to enjoy life and see his family happy.

- He's not very tech savvy, but uses a PC, which is also where he does most of his Internet browsing.

- His main pain points are things that cause him stress.

- His main goal is to live as long as possible, to enjoy life and ensure the well-being of his family.

- Gus gets most of his news offline through publications he subscribes to, like U-T San Diego and Wall Street Journal. On the Internet, he will read Fox News and any links to stories that family and friends share over email.

- His hobbies include: golf, travel, spending time with family and watching the San Diego sports teams.

Now that we've defined Gus, we can start to develop our golf business website around this customer persona.

To gear our site to him, we don't want to make our site too flashy. We want to make the font large enough and clean enough for him to easily read and the navigation to be straightforward. To allow him to confirm a reservation for a golf tee time, we may want to include the option to do that over the phone rather than via email.

Obviously, since we run a golf course, we want to include pictures illustrating the relaxing environment we provide, but we may also cater the images to Gus – pictures showing people who look like they could be him or his friends and maybe even include a few with multi-generational families (remember, he has four grandchildren).

Like all visitors, you want to capture his email address so you can market to him, but you might also figure out how to include his kids or grandkids and offer specials for family outings.

If you want to further market to him, you may have to think about targeting traditional media he may read like the U-T San Diego and Wall Street Journal.

Can you see how much easier it is to cater your site to your target market once you've defined a persona?

Not only that, but you'll see higher conversion rates (how often a visitor buys) when you scrutinize all of your content with your persona in mind.

Don't Play Hide and Seek

Usability is a key consideration when designing your site. Make it as easy as possible for visitors to find what they're looking for.

Have you ever been in a store and couldn't find what you were looking for? If so, it probably makes you want to leave (and you often do just walk out). The difference between searching for something in-person compared to online lies in the click of a mouse. If you travel to a store and have trouble finding something, you're going to put a lot more effort into looking than if you're just a quick web search away from getting what you need from a competitor.

Every website owner starts with the idea that their site is intuitive and easy to navigate, but is that really true? A big reason why website owners think this is because they helped design the structure of the site or at least approved of it.

Think of a website like your home. If someone asked you where in your kitchen you keep your forks, you might initially think that the answer is so intuitive, why would they even need to ask? But after thinking about it for a minute, you may realize that it's straightforward for you because of your familiarity with your kitchen and the fact that you most likely put them there in the first place.

Based on research by Usability.gov, a group funded by the US Government to study and determine best practices and guidelines for user experience (UX):
- About 50% of potential sales are lost because visitors can't find information they're searching for.
- Nearly 60% of the time, people cannot find what they're seeking on a website… at all.

Those are staggering numbers when you think about it. Losing half of all sales? Yikes, any bottom line will feel that hit eventually.

So what are some specific steps you can take to prevent that from happening on your site?

Put Things Where You'd Expect Them To Be

Make your navigation easy for users by locating a menu and search box near the top of your site. Don't make people have to hunt for these basic elements.

The main menu should be in an obvious location. It may look cool to do different things with your website's design that "break the mold," but be careful not to confuse people. A little attention and thought will help make sure that doesn't happen.

People have become accustomed to finding certain website elements, like a top menu and search box, in particular parts of the page (just like they do with ads). Why would you want to make them look for your menu and search box because they're not where they normally are for sites? That's like a retail store trying to be artistic and placing their entrance in a location that people wouldn't expect and worse, can't find.

Don't make your navigation menus too complex, either. Limit the options to seven or less on any level. Short-term memory limits people to only remembering about seven things at once – it can be overwhelming to have more options. If you have more than seven things that you want to link to from the top menu, it's better to have a drop down where people can see some additional links that are under the main menu options. For example, have an Electronics link on the top level, and then below that have links to Televisions, DVD Players, Cameras, Video Games, etc. (once again, don't have more than seven options here). Limit your menu to two levels deep, otherwise people will get lost.

Let's take a look at how Amazon.com, a site that has millions of pages, does it. They shrink their top-level menu options by combining high-level categories, such as Movies, Music & Games. Similarly, in their drop-down menu, they group like categories so you don't feel too overwhelmed with the choices (i.e. Camera, Photo & Video).

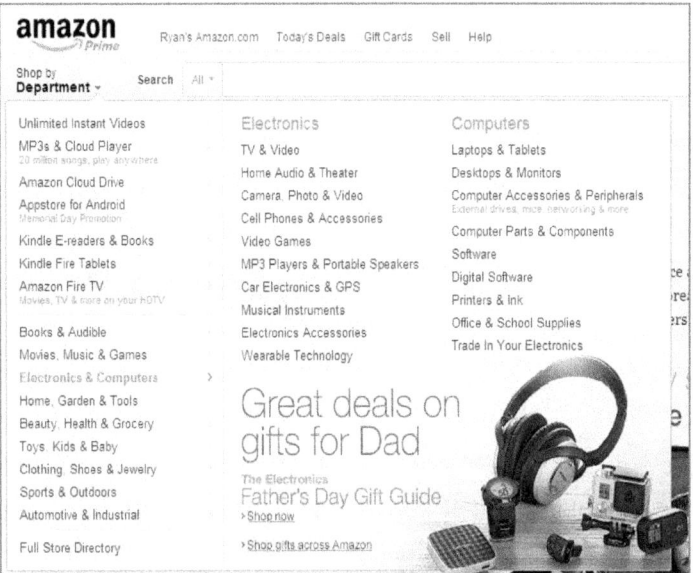

Once a visitor goes to (clicks) one of the category pages, like Camera, Photo & Video, they will see additional links on the side or below the main menu. You want to avoid hitting the person with all of these links at once. Even though it seems like they can get there with fewer clicks if you put every single link in the top menu, it's more likely that you'll overwhelm and frustrate them. Not to mention it will make your page very cluttered.

Here's another example from Nordstrom.com. Once you click on the menu to Men's > Boots, you are shown more navigation options to help narrow your search and pinpoint exactly the things you're interested in seeing.

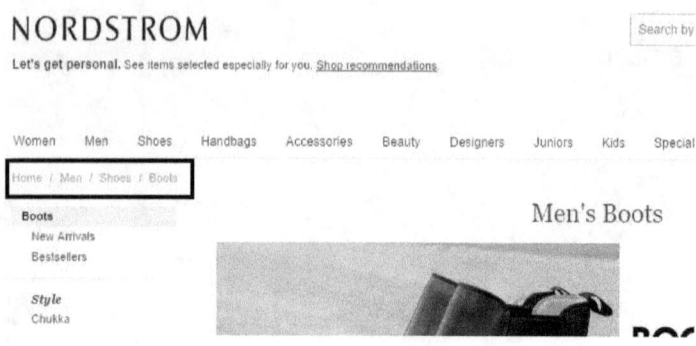

Hansel and Gretel

Now just because you're making navigation levels doesn't mean people won't still lose their way. They may be busily clicking away, but not really tracking how they're getting there. This is where you can again come to their rescue by building a breadcrumb trail for them.

Breadcrumb trails are another thing that makes user navigation easier. Think back to the story of Hansel and Gretel. They left a trail of breadcrumbs as they made their way through the forest so they could retrace their steps and find their way back home. You can do the same thing for visitors to your site... give users a way to find their way back to where they started.

Breadcrumbs are a series of links that show the path or steps the person took to get to this page (based on categories). It is characteristically found at the top of a page. It not only helps the user backtrack easier, but it also helps them easily visit pages related to this one.

On Costco.com, when you're on the page for Whirlpool® 4 Piece GAS Stainless Steel Side-by-Side Kitchen Suite, if you're not yet convinced this is what you want to buy, you can click the link for Kitchen Suites Gas to see alternatives. You can also navigate to a level higher than this, such as Appliances, if you want something altogether different.

"Eye" Don't Like Being Tired

Once you have figured out your navigation, you're ready to look at some of the aesthetics of a website. First and foremost, the words on a site should be easy to read.

Sure, fancier fonts can be stylish, but they can also be harder to read. Make sure any fonts on your site are large enough to understand immediately and not so fancy that it takes more effort to read them – too fancy, swirly, scrunched together, "clever," and so on. You don't want someone to have to decipher your content.

Common fonts that have the highest readability include Arial, Verdana and Georgia.

We're talking about fonts because you need to be concerned not only with people accurately reading the text, but also with those who may experience eye fatigue from putting too much strain and effort into reading your site. Eye fatigue changes the mood of the visitor (to a more unpleasant one) and, at least on a subconscious level, makes them more apt to leave.

Along those same lines, using too many font types on your site can also lead to eye fatigue - stick to three or less throughout your website (this is a good general practice for any type of marketing; you want to maintain continuity and cohesion and using too many fonts will lose both of those things).

The Tech Crunch and MSNBC pages shown below are two examples of very easy to read pages. They use large, clear fonts and a light black/grey for most of the smaller body copy so the contrast with the black background doesn't strain the eye too much.

Again, these are simple things you can do immediately to enhance the user experience on your site. Font choice will also have an impact on what we're going to talk about next, responsiveness.

Make Money on the Internet | 21

How Responsive Are You?

With people shifting their Internet viewing from desktops to mobile devices (i.e. smartphone, tablets, watches, glasses), it's important that your site is responsive.

Being responsive means that your site looks good and functions well regardless of what type of device a visitor is using to view your website. In other words, your site can adjust its look based on the type of device it's being viewed on – it responds to the device's screen specifications.

Not only is this crucial because you want visitors to have a great experience on your site regardless of how they're using it, but also because Google takes responsiveness into consideration in it's search algorithm.

This is where we start to look at your website structure beyond the user and into the bigger picture of overall performance.

If Google views your site as responsive, you'll rank higher in search results than if it isn't (all other things being equal). The reason that Google does this is because they believe in providing people with the best user results. This involves not only finding the most relevant content, but also identifying sites that will perform well – they show up (or "render") well regardless of the device being used and they don't take too long to load. As we're sure you can attest, it can be annoying if a site doesn't work well on a smartphone, or if a website takes a looooooooong time to load.

And what generally happens when you have to wait in the land of the Internet? You'll leave.

Below are some indications that a website is not responsive:

- You have to scroll from left to right to see all the content (it's too wide for a mobile device).
- You have to zoom in to read the text.
- Parts of the site don't fit on a page – like pop-up boxes.
- Text that is normally readable on a desktop becomes hard to read because it's not on the page or is being overlapped by some other element.

"Bootstrap" is a popular website design framework that is responsive. Here's how their main page looks when it's viewed on a desktop or laptop:

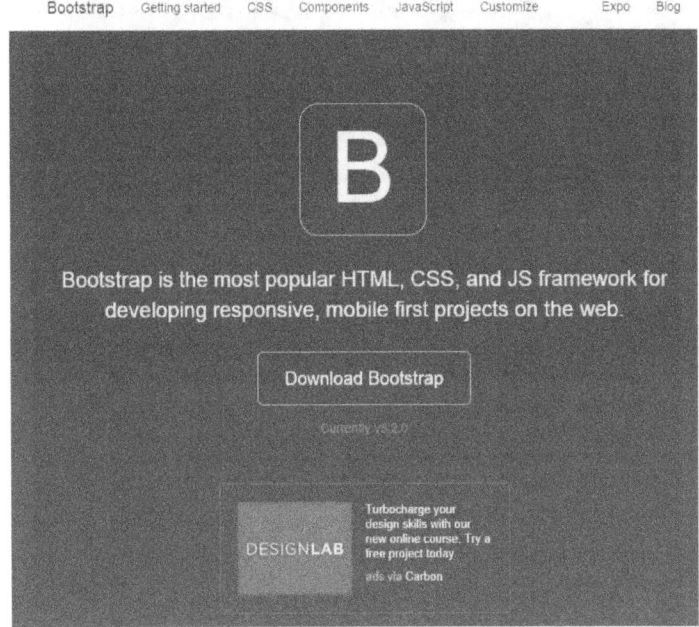

Next, look at how it appears on a smaller mobile device. You can see that the text menu disappears and it is now an icon in the upper right corner with the three horizontal lines (a universal Internet symbol for a menu). Also, the page becomes taller, with content aligning vertically instead of horizontally since mobile devices are more narrow – it's automatically adjusting based on the screen size.

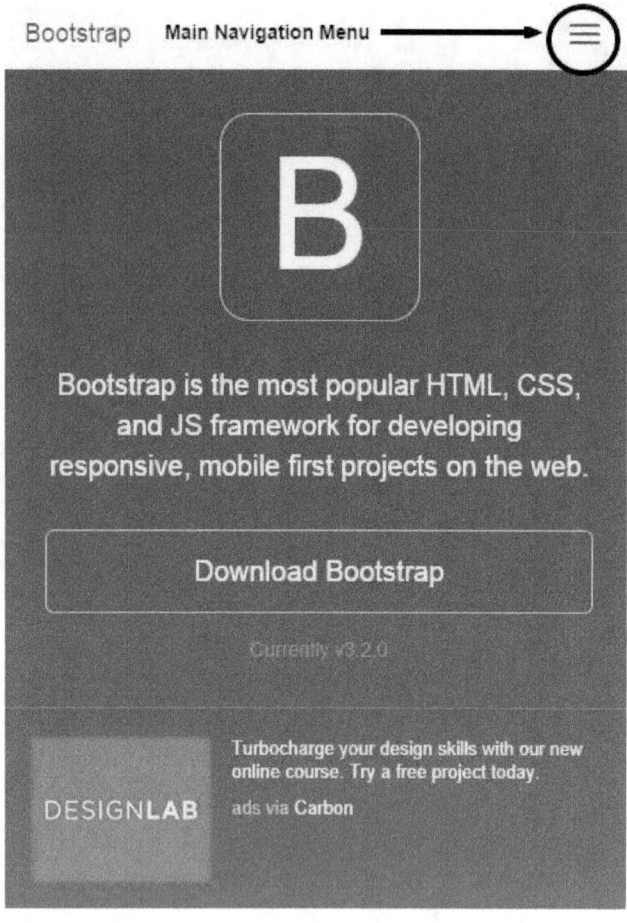

Making a site responsive is done through the code for your site that detects the width of the screen being used and changes the layout accordingly.

Once you have chosen a website design and start to build it out, you'll want to test how responsive it is and what it will look like on different devices.

Since it's highly unlikely that you have 30+ different types of devices to test your website on, there are some free web apps that you can use to simulate what it's like to view your site on different devices. Two really good ones are Am I Responsive and Responsinator.

Aside from how a site appears, you also want to ensure that all of the features work on different devices. For example, Flash doesn't work on Apple devices (iOS operating system), so if you used it on your site, unless your website is coded to do something else in place of the Flash when it is viewed on an iPhone or iPad, the visitor will see an empty black space.

Also, be sure that anything that triggers when a mouse hovers over it on desktops (like drop down menus) work on mobile devices as well – often they don't. Unfortunately for testing this, you have to do it with actual devices. At a minimum, if you don't have devices across different platforms, enlist the help of a friend to test your site using mobile devices with Android, iOS and Windows to make sure that the functionality works across the board.

1: Resources

Responsive Design

Am I Responsive (http://ami.responsivedesign.is) – Check how your site looks across different devices to see if it is responsive.

Responsinator (http://www.responsinator.com/) – Check how your site looks across different devices to see if it is responsive.

Website Design Information

Usability.gov (http://usability.gov) – Recommendations on best practices for website usability based on research conducted by the US government.

WhatFont (http://chengyinliu.com/whatfont.html) – A free browser plugin that allows you to easily see what font is being used on any web page. So if you come across one you like, you can see what it is and use it on your own site.

1: Your Actionable Checklist

- Have you defined at least one customer persona?
- Have you kept your persona in mind and thought about how they would personally react to each page on your site?
- Do you have a menu and search box near the top of the page, right where people would expect it to be?
- Do you have too many menu options?
- Is the style of your font easy to read?
- Are your fonts big enough to read?
- Are you using, at most, three font styles on your site?
- Does your site force visitors to scroll or zoom in when viewing it on a mobile device?
- Have you tested your site across different mobile operating systems (Android, iOS and Windows) to ensure that everyone has a similar experience and things don't seem to be broken?

[2]

Do You Trust Me?

Now that we've looked at some of the very basics of successful web selling – the starting points – let's talk about building trust and your reputation.

Next to being able to find information that they need to buy your product or service, the most important factor for a customer is whether they think they can trust you. How much does it really matter that you're selling the best product in the world if the person doesn't think that they can trust you?

Not at all.

A visitor will not buy from you if they think that you might:
- Take their money and run.
- Give them a product that is inferior to what they're learning about on your site (bait and switch).
- Lose their personal and payment information if your site is hacked.
- Sell their contact information to third parties.

- Spam them.

Yes, It's Personal

One of the best things you can do to get people to trust you is to allow them to get to know you personally.

You want to try to get people to like you. Show pictures of yourself, as well as employees of the company. Tell them the history of your company and why you started the business. Show pictures of people, along with their bio. Better yet, show a video of that person speaking about themselves. In the bios, include relevant work experience that demonstrates expertise, and also personal tidbits that make them more human (hobbies, why they like what they do, whether they are married, have kids or pets, etc.).

Once someone gets to know you, it builds trust. They feel more comfortable that you will treat them fairly and not steal their money because they can identify with you. You're not some big business that may treat them like they're an anonymous order number or simply dollars and cents. You're less likely to be seen as a scammer sitting in a basement throwing up generic websites and taking people's money.

Call Me, Maybe

Along with letting people get to know you and your company on a more personal level, you want to let people know that you're accessible.

The best way to do this is to **make sure you have your phone number and address on your website**. This is going to serve two purposes. It will help advance you in local search results and build confidence that you're a legit business. When a website only offers a contact form or an email address, it may make visitors wonder, *"Why are they making it so hard for me to contact them? Is it so I can't find them if a purchase goes bad?"*

There is one more benefit to having your address and phone number on your site. It makes it more likely that a customer will actually contact you, thereby increasing your chance for a sale.

If possible, place your phone number on every page of your site. An easy way to do this is to place it in your footer. The address you provide should be a legitimate physical location. PO Boxes and Private Mail Boxes (PMB) shouldn't be used as your sole address because that gives the impression you're trying to hide (although they can be used as a supplemental mailing address, if you prefer to have mail delivered there).

You should also include a **map**, such as Google Maps, on your Contact Us page, so people can see how to get to your location. Adding **pictures** of your location can also increase trust.

The bottom line for taking these extra steps is that it gives people comfort to know there's a place they can physically visit to talk to you, even though the chances of them actually doing so is small.

If you're a really small business, like a one-person shop or if you work out of your home, you may not want to provide your cell phone number or home address on your site. In those cases, we recommend using **virtual phone and mail services.**

A **virtual phone service** gives the illusion of being a bigger company by offering a toll-free number, call forwarding (to your cell phone), call transferring (to a coworker), Internet fax, and voicemail. In fact, you can even opt for the automated prompts that say, "For X, press or say 1; for Y, press or say 2…" Ring Central is a paid service you can use for this purpose. If you can do without all of the bells and whistles and just want to have a different phone number with voicemail, take a look at Google Voice.

If you work primarily from home, consider establishing a **virtual mailbox.** Virtual mailboxes allow you to receive mail with addresses that don't include "PO Box" or "PMB" in them. It's not a perfect solution because if someone looks at a map they will see another business, but it will provide a physical address without the worry of having your dinner interrupted if a customer were to show up at your door. Earth Class Mail is a service that will let you set up you a virtual mailbox in different cities.

Having a virtual mailbox can also be helpful if you want to give the impression that your business is "local," but you don't have a physical presence in that particular geographic area. For example, if you live in Seattle and want to offer accounting services in an area where you don't have an office, like Los Angeles, Earth Class Mail can give you that local "presence."

This Is No Time For Amateur Hour

While we did say earlier that beautiful websites aren't the most important thing when designing an online destination, the actual look really does matter. You want a professional looking design – one that doesn't look too cluttered, cookie cutter or amateur.

Just think about how you feel when you step into a business where things look old and cheap – peeling paint, dirty fixtures or bathrooms, worn out furniture, outdated carpet – compared to one that looks cleaner, newer, more well cared for. You typically have more trust in the business that looks nicer because subconsciously, you know that it takes more effort to outfit and maintain their place like this, which means that they're earning more from their customers than their competitor, perhaps. It also shows that they're paying attention to the impression they are having on their customers.

The same is true with websites. You want to let visitors know that you're concerned that they have a positive experience on your site and you are conscientious enough to invest time, energy and money to make sure that happens.

While there are a ton of free tools and services out there that you could use to build your own site, sometimes it's worth it to pay a little more to have it done right, especially if you've never done it before. Two resources we like are Squarespace and Shopify. They offer easy to use website hosting and building tools that have built-in professional looking designs.

Yes, you will need to pay a little bit of money. But you have control over that expense and depending on your needs, you can establish a really nice, functioning website on a small budget or you can certainly spend thousands of dollars with a professional web designer. That is completely up to you, but just know that there are effective options to suit just about any budget.

What Would Others Do (WWOD)?

So what are some other ways to build trust and boost your reputation?

Testimonials and reviews are a great way to build trust with customers because they offer the opinion of others just like them. **Testimonials** are positive comments that customers have about your services/products, while **reviews** are good and bad opinions that people have about your services/products.

Since testimonials can easily be fabricated, you'll want to make sure to provide enough details that visitors are convinced that this is most likely the opinion of a real person. Video testimonials are the most convincing, but if you can't do that, then make sure you accompany their comments with:
- A photo of the testimonial provider.
- First and last name (or at least a last initial, such as Mary L.).
- Where they live (city, state or country, if applicable).

A company name and title can also help with credibility. For example, when this person's job gives their opinion additional credence, like a doctor who is commenting on a health product.

Angie's List is one company/website built completely on trust. It provides reviews on service providers to paid members. If people don't trust that Angie's List is providing accurate, neutral, reliable information, then the business has no customers. Therefore, trust is everything to Angie's List.

Here's what the testimonial page on Angie's List looks like:

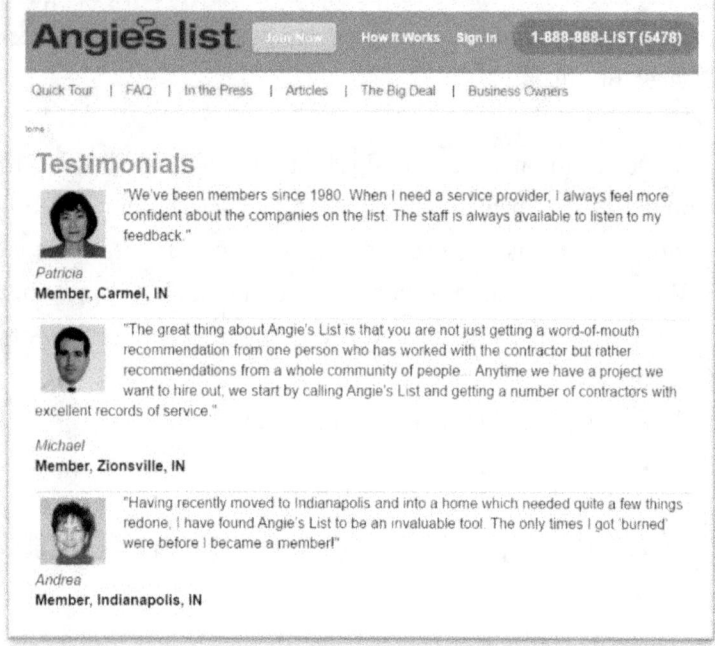

For **reviews**, you again want to make sure that people believe that they are real. Like testimonials, reviews can easily be faked – for good or evil purposes. If people think that the reviews are doctored, including them on your website may have actually have a adverse impact on visitors.

Whatever you do, do not delete or ignore negative reviews (unless they contain foul language or are spam). Your instinct might be to get rid of them and only post positive ones, but let us explain.

Website owners are often hesitant to include reviews, in general, because they're afraid of the negative ones. You inevitably will get negative reviews. The nice thing about negative reviews is that even though they can be unpleasant to read, you can learn from them. You will be able to learn about things that your customers don't like and adjust your product/service offerings to fix them for subsequent customers. You can even write a comment back to the reviewer, responding to them publicly by thanking them for their feedback and letting them know that you've made changes so this issue does not occur again.

This shows customers that you care about them. It also shows **a level of transparency** that can lead to confidence and comfort for customers. They may want to do business with you since you're not hiding anything.

To combat negative reviews, you want to encourage people to leave more reviews. Unfortunately, people are less compelled to comment when they are satisfied with a purchase (compared to when they are angry about one). So you want to encourage people to leave feedback more often since most of your customers will have had a good experience.

Some ways to encourage feedback are to post signs in your store (if you have a physical location), print reminders to leave a review on packing slips or receipts, send automated emails after delivery to ask for a review, or hold contests (randomly selected winner) where anyone who leaves a review is automatically entered into a contest to win some sort of prize.

For many people, whenever they think about buying a product the first place they go is Amazon.com. We trust that their reviews are, for the most part, genuine (since there are third party sellers on the site, some may create fake reviews to improve sales and sometimes their competitors may leave false negatives to hurt sales). The reviews are trustworthy because they indicate when a reviewer actually made a purchase ("verified purchase"), allow you to see the other reviews by that reviewer (so you know someone isn't creating all the reviews with a few dummy accounts) and you will see plenty of negative reviews.

When thumbing through the reviews on Amazon, think about:
- The quantity of reviews (for a product).
- The overall rating (how many stars out of five).
- How many of the reviews are verified purchases (you know they actually bought the product before making a review).
- The worst things that people have to say about the product.

Customer Reviews

★★★★★ (3,751)
4.3 out of 5 stars

5 star	2,438
4 star	621
3 star	232
2 star	183
1 star	277

It is easy to clean.
Prime Reviewer

I have used the panini side of the plates for making sandwiches and the griddle side for pancakes, and both work well.
n:o567

Steaks, bacon, burgers, pork chops, fish, chicken breasts, and grilled burritos all come out great!
Boilermate

See all 3,751 customer reviews

Most Helpful Customer Reviews

2,133 of 2,170 people found the following review helpful
★★★★★ **Cuisinart upgraded the Griddler, and it's better than ever**
By S. Harrison TOP 1000 REVIEWER   VINE VOICE on February 27, 2010

Vine Customer Review of Free Product (What's this?)

I bought a G4 Griddler from Amazon in 2005, and used it a couple of times a week (at least) until it had to be put out to pasture in 2010 due to failure of the non-stick coating on the plates. (The coating started to bubble and peel, and no one wants that in their food...) I loved it. (See my review of the Cuisinart GR-4 Griddler Stainless-Steel 4-in-1 Grill/Griddle and Panini Press) it was still working great, but replacement plates were not available.

I was elated when offered the opportunity to review its smarter younger brother, the GR-4NAM Griddler. I could hardly wait for it to get here and run it through its paces.

At first glance, the GR-4NAM looks virtually identical to the G4. However, closer inspection reveals that it has been totally redesigned, and for the better.

Do reviews impact what you buy? What, in particular, catches your attention in a review?

Think about your answers to those questions and try to incorporate them into your site.

Trustees

Another way to get third parties to vouch for you is to sign up for services that offer a specific type of endorsement for you. You've probably seen these many times and may not even pay attention to them anymore.

Common types of endorsements are **badges** given to signify that you can be trusted and that your site is secure. You may think that only smaller businesses need this, but that's not the case. Even large, well-known brands use these types of endorsements.

Here are just a few examples:

Buy.com (on the bottom of pages) shows Bizrate, Trustwave and Google Trusted Store badges in the footer:

Overstock.com shows the Norton Secured (Verisign) logo at checkout:

BestBuy.com (on the bottom of pages) shows the TRUSTe badge in lower right corner:

Most of these services are paid, with the exception of the Google Trusted Store badge. Understand that the more popular the service is (like Google), the more powerful it is.

If you are going to include a badge on your site, put them in a place on your website that makes sense. This means placing them where someone will see them when they typically might have a particular concern.

From the examples above, you can see that you might place a trust badge in your footer so it shows up on every page to answer the question, "Can I trust this company?" Then you may include the secure badge on your checkout pages, when the question may crop up, "Is my payment safe?" If you have a badge showing your site is secure, sometimes you may not want to show it too early in the buying process because it may raise (instead of alleviate) questions of security, "Why are they showing me this now?"

To know for sure, it's always best to run what's called an A/B test. That is to say, see what your conversion rate is (how often visitors buy) when a secure badge is on every page, as opposed to just on the checkout pages. You're testing one option, "A," against another, "B" to see which one performs better. Once you have a significant enough number of results to make a decision, place the badge on whichever option gets the higher conversion rate – more sales.

I'm Gonna Make You An Offer You Can't Refuse

Visitors face a certain amount of fear when they're shopping. They have worked hard for their money and want to get a good value for it - they're scared of losing their money.

Aside from doing things to build up your trust reputation, you can employ a technique used in marketing called "**risk reversal**." Risk reversal is *making an offer that places some of the risk on the seller*, as opposed to all of it on the buyer. This helps provide comfort in the online shopping experience.

Some examples of offers you can make include:
- 30 Day Money Back Guarantee
- Free Trial
- Low Price Guarantee (you'll match competitor prices)
- Free Shipping

Similar to trust badges, make sure that your offer is displayed prominently – don't hide it. In fact, ensure that almost every page, if not *every* page, has the offer on it (preferably near the top).

Examples of displaying the offer (which are usually displayed with an eye-catching graphic and link to a page that explains more details on the offer) are as follows:

Walmart.com - Free Shipping offer

BestBuy.com - Low price guarantee

NatureMade.com - Love Them or They're Free

Rules Aren't Meant To Be Broken

Be as transparent on your website as possible to your visitors so they know what to expect.

Surprises often upset people, especially during the buying process. To reduce the possibility of any surprises, include a list of your policies or Frequently Asked Questions (FAQs) to let your customers know the standards and processes your business has established. This not only helps reduce the amount of customer service inquiries you receive, but also puts buyers at ease because they know what to expect from you.

Some common types of website policies include:

1. **Privacy Policy** – Indicates what type of information is gathered from someone when they come to your site, how it's used and who has access to it.
2. **Terms and Conditions** – These communicate what you are providing on your site, any limitations of the site, what the user is allowed to do when using the site, and what happens if something goes wrong when someone uses the site.
3. **Help/FAQs**
    a. **Return/Refund Policy** – When is a buyer eligible for a return/refund, how do they request one and which items are eligible?
    b. **Shipping Policy** – How quickly do items ship, how fast should a buyer expect to receive something?

Place links to your policies on every page, in a location that they expect to see them (usually at the bottom of the page) so they're easy to find.

Believe it or not, NOT having these things on your site may stand out more to visitors because while we may not specifically read all of these policies, we notice if they're not there. Failing to build them into your site can end up costing you a sale.

2: Resources

Website Building Software

Shopify (http://shopify.com) – A service you can use to build professional looking websites for a low monthly fee.

Squarespace (http://squarespace.com) – A service you can use to build professional looking websites for a low monthly fee.

Trust Tools

Better Business Bureau Online (http://bbb.org/online) – Join the Better Business Bureau and include the code that they provide for a badge (which links to your BBB record and grade) to build trust.

Bizrate (http://bizrate.com) – A paid service that allows customers to leave ecommerce site reviews. Site owners can obtain a badge to include on their website.

Earth Class Mail (http://earthclassmail.com) – A way to provide a physical mailing location that is not a PO Box.

Google Maps (http://maps.google.com) – A free map that you can embed on your Contact page so people can see where you're located.

Google Trusted Store (http://www.google.com/trustedstores/) – A free certification program from Google that allows you to put a Google Trusted Stores badge on your site.

Google Voice (www.google.com/voice) – A free service that provides a telephone number and voicemail for your business

Ring Central (http://www.ringcentral.com/) – A virtual phone service that lets you appear like you're a bigger business by offering complete telephone service with call forwarding, automated attendant, Internet fax, voicemail, call transfer, call screening, and paging.

Survey Monkey (http://surveymonkey.com) – Free software you can use to conduct online surveys of your customers.

TRUSTe (http://truste.com) – Provides a badge to paid members who pass a privacy assessment conducted by TRUSTe.

Verisign (http://www.verisign.com) – One of many SSL providers. This one is more expensive than most, but is one of the most recognized ads for security.

2: Actionable Checklist

- Can people get to know you via your website?
- Do you have ways for people to contact you beyond a contact form?
- Can you integrate third party badges/images that will boost your credibility with site visitors?
- Are you showing testimonials/reviews from customers that other visitors can read or watch (videos)?
- Are there any trust signs you can use that you aren't already?
- How can you remove the risk for customers?
- Do you clearly state your policies (refunds and returns, privacy policy, terms and conditions, etc.) on your website?

[3]

The Purpose Driven Page

If you want to create an online selling machine (which we're assuming you do since you're reading this book), each page on your website should serve a purpose and somehow move a visitor closer to making a purchase from you. Together, these pages are your web selling building blocks. What you need to do is take each page and determine what its purpose will be – how they will work together to drive you to your goal.

Some pages will be geared to providing information outside of your products/services, like general information about your company. This means things like About Us, a map/driving directions and policy pages (terms and conditions, privacy policy, frequently asked questions).

However, with most pages, you want to direct visitors toward taking a specific action that moves them closer to making a purchase. On pages that describe your product/service, direct them to a button that allows them to make a purchase or to give you some sort of contact information (thereby becoming a lead).

While that may seem intuitive on retail sites that have individual product pages where you're trying to get the people to click the Add to Cart button, websites often forget to place a Call To Action (CTA – spurring a visitor to take some sort of action; to do something) in other places where they should have one.

If one CTA is a good thing, multiple CTAs is even better, right? Wrong.

One challenge that many business owners face is having too many CTAs on a page. In fact, this is the reason why many websites don't result in the number of sales or leads as they should. Having more than one CTA can lead to confusion – visitors won't know which one to do. It's a balancing act between guiding someone to take an action, but not giving them so many options for things to do that it takes traffic from your ultimate goal of getting a sale.

In this section, we'll analyze your site using analytics to see how effective it is at fulfilling each page's purpose, how to use CTAs and how to design your site so that you're converting visitors to customers as often as possible.

Goooooooooooooooooooooaaaaaall!!!

Mrs Gemstone. "Hockey - Goal!! Crowd reaction to the goal scored." 10 Mar 2010. Online image. Flickr. 27 May 2014. <https://www.flickr.com/photos/gemstone/4432041243/>

Before you start to optimize your pages to get higher conversion rates, you need to make sure that you have the tools in place to track how effective the site is overall.

Your first step needs to be Google Analytics. Google Analytics has become the leading tool for tracking website data for a number of reasons: it's free, easy to install and provides valuable reporting. The basic reports (50+ reports are included with every account) provide lots of useful information, but you can also develop your own reports or use ones that others have created.

To start using Google Analytics, sign-up for a free account on their site at www.google.com/analytics. Once you sign up, you will be given a small snippet of code to add to the backend of your website. If you are adept at updating your own website you should be able to do this yourself, or have your website developer add it in for you if you're unsure. The tracking code will send anonymous visitor data (it doesn't identify who the visitor is, just information about them) back to Google each time someone visits the page.

Once you have the snippet of code installed, the next thing to think about is, what are your goals for the site? Obviously you need to track sales and/or leads, so you want to record whenever you reach one of those as goals. But don't forget about the "small yeses."

"Small yeses" are actions the visitor takes that inch them closer to becoming a customer. Some examples include: clicking on a button to go to a landing page, filling out a contact form or using a live chat function to ask questions.

Some other "small yeses" may be when a visitor:
- Stays on a page or the site for a certain number of minutes
- Visits a particular page
- Plays a video on a page
- Registers for an event
- Clicks a button
- Shares something
- Visits a certain number of pages

Once you figure out what you want to define as goals, you set them up in Google Analytics. Then, whenever a goal is reached, it will be recorded as a **conversion** in Google Analytics. Now you'll be able to see how often a conversion happens (i.e. how often a visitor completes a predetermined goal) and learn what sites or links direct (bring) the most converted visitors to your site; you'll see where they're coming from.

In Analytics, you can even assign a dollar amount to a goal. For example, if you know that when someone plays a video, 10% of the time they will make a $150 purchase, you might assign a $15 value ($150 x .10) for that goal. Think of it in terms of a lead and how that lead is worth a certain amount of money based on how often you can close the sale and how much profit an average purchase nets.

Depending on the goal and what event triggers it on your site, you set them up in different ways. Let's look at an example.

Here we'll show you how to set one a goal for a hot tub business, Julie's Hot Tubs. Hot tubs are a "big ticket product" – they cost a fair amount of money, and you have a significantly higher chance of closing the sale if you get to talk to the prospect. Plus, prices are often not shown on the website. These are expensive items, aren't impulse buys and usually require more convincing for the person to purchase (as opposed to more inexpensive products). In this and similar cases, the best way to generate sales is to get the person to provide their contact information using a lead incentive (we'll go more into lead incentives later) so you can personally follow-up with them via phone or email.

Here's what we know about Julie's Hot Tubs:
- Average hot tub purchase: $7,000
- Product for average sale costs: $4,000
- When we get a lead online, we can close 5% of the time

Knowing that data, we can determine the profit from an average sale is $3,000 ($7,000-$4,000). We can also determine that a website lead is worth $150 ($3,000 x .05). We can use this information in setting up our goal in Google Analytics (this is optional, but it's good to track if you know the information).

To capture the contact information of the visitor, there is a web form that they fill out and submit before they receive the lead incentive (sit tight, we're getting to that). After submitting the form, they are taken to a Thank You page to confirm that we received their information and to express our appreciation for completing the form.

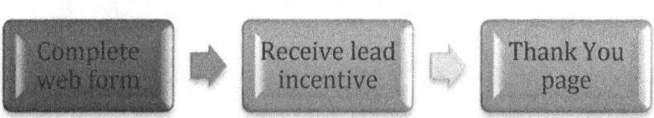

Here's how we create the goal in Google Analytics for recording a lead:

1. Log in to your Google Analytics account.
2. Click on the *Admin* link on the top menu:

3. Under *Website Data*, click Goals:

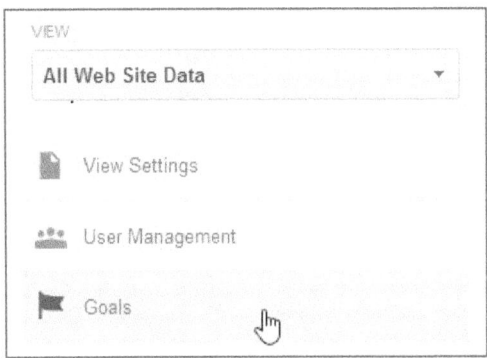

4. On the Goals dashboard, click *New Goal* button:

5. In the Goal setup section, click the button next to *Contact Us*, and then click *Next Step*:

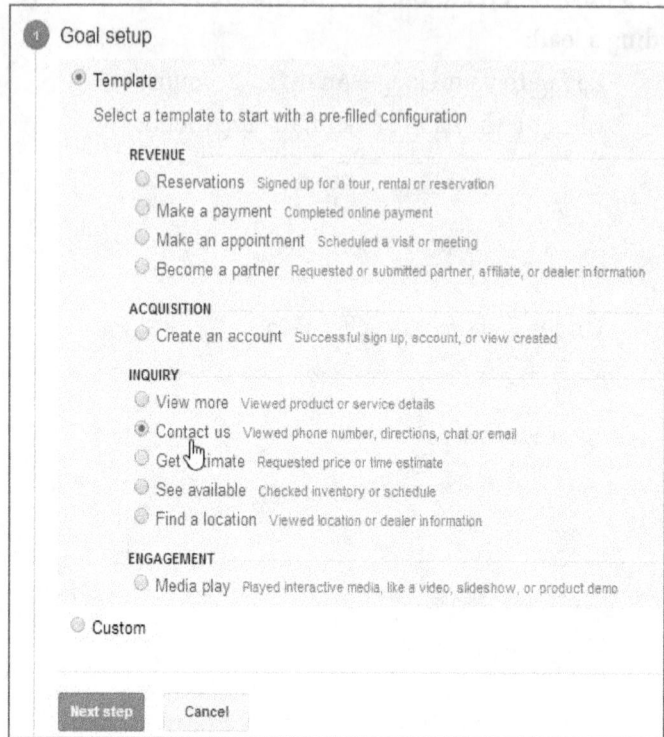

6. In the Goal description section, give your goal a name, select *Destination,* and then click *Next step*:

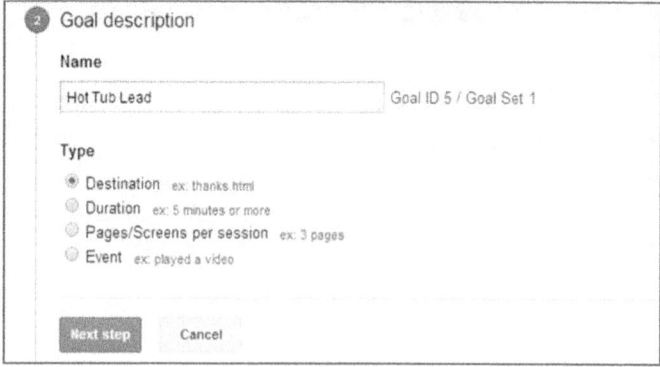

7. In the Goal details section, fill in the field under *Destination* using the web address of the Thank You page (julieshottubs.com/thanks.html). We only have to put the part of the address after the domain name (i.e. /thanks.html). Also, turn the Value tracking on and assign 150 for it (the amount that represents the value of an online lead to us), and then click *Create Goal*.

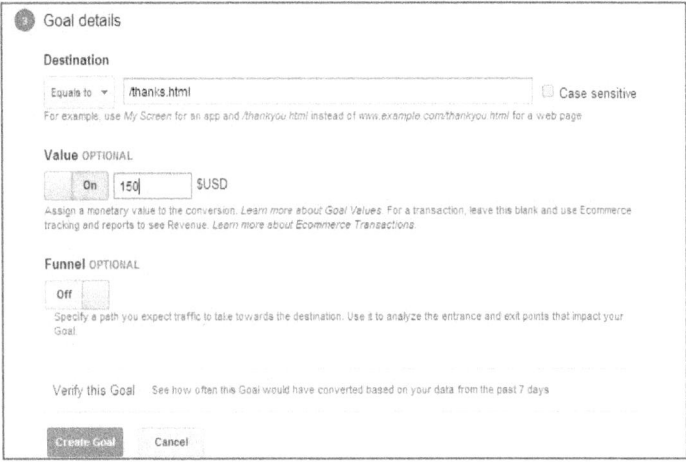

Voilà! Google Analytics will now report any goal conversions for future traffic (it does not go back to any visitors who have been to your site prior to setting up this goal).

After you're done with the set-up, the reports will tell you:
- How frequently visitors are turning into leads or customers.
- What traffic sources and keywords are the most profitable.

- What traffic sources and keywords lead to sales most often.
- Where people might be dropping off (leaving the site) before becoming a lead or customer.

Here's a sample of the reporting related to conversions:

1. See how often certain keywords become sales.

Keyword	Sessions	% New Sessions	New Users	Bounce Rate	Pages / Session	Avg. Session Duration	Transactions	Revenue	Ecommerce Conversion Rate
	6,025 % of Total: 19.62% (30 687)	61.31% Site Avg: 60.92% (0.72%)	3,694 % of Total: 19.33% (19,308)	24.81% Site Avg: 27.79% (-10.67%)	4.34 Site Avg: 3.62 (20.00%)	00:03:49 Site Avg: 00:02:44 (39.67%)	133 % of Total: 27.31% (487)	$15,885.40 % of Total: 29.01% ($53,200.80)	2.21% Site Avg: 1.39% (58.12%)
1		4,925 (81.74%)	61.76%	3,042 (82.35%)	25.64%	4.30	00:03:43	98 (73.68%)	$12,006.65 (75.58%)	1.99%
2		230 (3.82%)	51.74%	119 (3.22%)	14.78%	4.81	00:03:29	11 (8.27%)	$1,037.75 (6.53%)	4.78%
3		161 (2.67%)	60.87%	98 (2.65%)	12.42%	5.01	00:04:01	7 (5.26%)	$529.65 (3.33%)	4.35%
4		80 (1.33%)	78.75%	63 (1.71%)	8.75%	4.40	00:04:40	2 (1.50%)	$346.00 (2.18%)	2.50%
5		44 (0.73%)	54.55%	24 (0.65%)	22.73%	4.05	00:03:58	1 (0.75%)	$79.00 (0.50%)	2.27%
6		44 (0.73%)	61.36%	27 (0.73%)	13.64%	5.27	00:04:59	2 (1.50%)	$168.00 (1.06%)	4.55%
7		40 (0.66%)	50.00%	20 (0.54%)	27.50%	6.30	00:07:06	1 (0.75%)	$99.00 (0.62%)	2.50%
8		29 (0.48%)	58.62%	17 (0.46%)	6.90%	3.17	00:02:54	0 (0.00%)	$0.00 (0.00%)	0.00%
9		9 (0.15%)	88.89%	8 (0.22%)	22.22%	1.44	00:00:21	0 (0.00%)	$0.00 (0.00%)	0.00%
10		9 (0.15%)	0.00%	0 (0.00%)	33.33%	3.00	00:01:14	0 (0.00%)	$0.00 (0.00%)	0.00%

2. See which sources send you the most conversions.

Goals			
Goal Completion Location			
Source / Medium	Source / Medium	Goal Completions	% Goal Completions
	1. google / organic	70	19.94%
	2. (direct) / (none)	64	18.23%
	3. google / cpc	64	18.23%
	4. hs_email / email	42	11.97%
	5. shareasale.com / referral	26	7.41%
	6. facebook / cpc	18	5.13%
	7. bing / cpc	13	3.70%
	8. bing / organic	10	2.85%
	9. hs_automation / email	9	2.56%
	10. perfectaudience / cpc	6	1.71%

view full report

3. See how many conversions were sent from social media.

Social Network	Conversions	Conversion Value
	18	$1,055.15
	% of Total: 2.15% (838)	% of Total: 1.98% ($53,264.80)
1. Facebook	10 (55.56%)	$712.00 (67.48%)
2. Twitter	4 (22.22%)	$164.05 (15.55%)
3. Facebook Apps	2 (11.11%)	$99.00 (9.38%)
4. Pinterest	2 (11.11%)	$80.10 (7.59%)

Aside from telling you how successful you are at converting visitors into customers, Google Analytics can tell you:
- Who is visiting your site (the demographics, their location, the device they used to access your site, their interests)
- How people are finding your site (search engines, social networks, paid ads, sites that link to you)
- What keywords visitors are interested in
- What content people are sharing on social media and how often

That's just a taste of the wealth of information that Google Analytics can help you learn about your traffic and visitor behavior. Signing up for Google Analytics or some form of website reporting is crucial if you want to learn how well your website is performing.

Then you can fine-tune it to make it as profitable as possible.

What's A Landing Page?

A landing page, also occasionally referred to as a squeeze page, is a specific type of page within a website that has the sole purpose of generating a lead or a sale.

For businesses selling products, the page will focus only on selling a particular product. For service-oriented (or big ticket product) businesses, they will often contain a form for obtaining a potential client, customer or patient's information – name, email address and phone number – to generate a lead that can be followed up on.

Since a landing page has only one goal, it is very effective in generating leads and sales.

Now, you as a website owner may say, "But I have plenty of pages that have this information on it."

It's true that many web pages can have such information and may appear to be landing pages. Let's say that you're a healthcare provider and you have pages describing your services. They would contain a lot of the aforementioned information that a landing page would have.

One of the biggest distinctions comes down to CTAs, or what you want a visitor to do on a certain page. The more obvious your CTA is, the higher your conversion rates are likely to be.

A **conversion** occurs when someone completes one of your CTAs, while the **conversion rate** is how often a visitor does it. The conversions most businesses are interested in are when a visitor buys a product (sale), submits a form (lead) or contacts them (lead).

Let's dig a little deeper into what a successful landing page looks like.

Elements of a Successful Landing Page

In order to design an effective landing page, you have to first determine what your goal is.

Some examples of goals are getting someone to:
- Complete a web form.
- Call a phone number.
- Buy a certain product.
- Register for an event (i.e. webinar, seminar).

Remember... pick only one goal, otherwise your landing page will lose effectiveness with too many CTAs and you run the risk of confusing your visitors. You can always get a prospect to do other things down the line once you have their contact information, but for now, focus on one thing to increase the odds they will take the steps you want them to take.

Next, you want to think about what your message will be. Consider how you'll gain **attention, interest, desire and action (AIDA)** from your site visitor. Once you've decided on what you'll say, you'll design the page and again include more analytics for constant optimization.

Meet AIDA

A website visitor goes through a process before making a purchase. Think about your own online researching or purchasing habits.

At a minimum, a visitor needs to know how a product/service will help them, whether the benefits they will receive are worth the cost and why you are the right business to buy from.

Once you have someone looking at your landing page, you don't want to squander the opportunity that their attention presents. Someone shopping via the web is likely to look at multiple sites, so make sure that you: (1) make a great first impression that resonates with them and (2) usher them through the buying decision as far as you can.

A simple way to think about guiding the person to make a purchase from you is to focus on getting their Attention, Interest, Desire, and Action (AIDA).

Attention
First you want to get their **Attention**. Summarize the main benefit of your offering in one headline that grabs their attention. Make it compelling enough so they want to continue reading.

If possible, use an image or a video to attract the person's attention. This is a powerful way to draw a viewer's eyes, and a way to show them how you will help them or explain that this offering is relevant to them.

Another thing that grabs the attention of viewers are logos that provide credibility – media outlets you've been featured in, associations you're a part of, certifications/standards you meet, or perhaps names/logos of existing customers. These logos build trust with viewers, especially if they are readily recognizable.

Interest
Next, draw their **Interest**. Telling a compelling story is a great way to do this. The more relatable you make the story to the visitor, the better. You want to pique this person's interest by making the story applicable to them. Make sure and illustrate the pain points - the problems or issues that need to be fixed.

Desire
Spur their **Desire**. Once you've done this, communicate what the big benefit is that you will provide. Also, sell the vision of what it will be like once they receive your offering. If you're selling a health product, you may want to emphasize things like: how much more energetic the customer will feel, how much more relaxed they could be or how their pain may disappear. Then paint a vision of something your clients may like, such as being able to spend more time with their grandchildren or to live an active lifestyle again.

Your product or service by itself is not what your prospective customer seeks. They ultimately want the change in their life that it can bring.

When you're thinking about how you'll convey this vision, don't limit yourself to just text. Video often has the highest conversion rates – it is the type of content that most often drives people to take action.

Action
Finally, drive them to **Action**. After convincing the person that your product or service can help lead them to a positive change they need or want, it's time to get them to act. All of your signs and messaging should lead them towards the goal you already defined. If you're selling a product that is inexpensive, you can push for the immediate sale. In many cases, your potential buyer may not be ready to give your their money just yet.

In the case of a high priced item or service, they may have to think about the purchase some more, which is to be expected. That's OK. Again, this is a buying process filled with many decisions, not only one. Just because they aren't ready to buy yet doesn't mean you should sit idly by while they make their decision. Instead you want to continue to guide them through the process.

In the situations where your buyers are more apt to take some time before making a purchase on the spot, focus on capturing the lead instead of pushing for the sale immediately. This way, you can follow-up with the prospect.

People are naturally hesitant to give out their contact information, so you have to provide a good reason why they should do so. Often the best way is with a bribe for something of value, such as a free eBook (inexpensive for you to produce but valuable to them). This not only gets you their contact details, but moves them toward the buying decision by providing education on what your service or product can do for them.

We'll cover these bribes, or **lead incentives**, more in depth in the next step.

Laying It All Out

Just as important as your messaging is how you say it (visually).

As we mentioned earlier, you want to avoid having too many calls to action on any given page. That means your pages will not all have the same framework, which is ok. There are things you just don't want to include on your landing page. For example, leave the navigation links to parts of your website (Contact Us, About Us, etc.) off of the landing page. These simply serve as distractions that will prevent your prospect from completing your desired goal.

They will see those navigational elements once they have gone past the landing page.

With that said, here are some things that you do want to include:

Headline – This is a concise statement that clearly articulates the biggest benefit a person will receive from using your product/service. When you're driving traffic to the landing page, keep in mind that the headline you use needs to match the source, if it doesn't, your conversion rate will be lower than it should be.

For example, if you have a Google ad that links to the page and that says, "Buy High Quality Widgets," but your headline is "The Lowest Priced Widgets Anywhere... Guaranteed!" your conversion rate will suffer. It may sound to you like they both say the same thing, but that may not be the case for a visitor. People don't like being surprised when they click on links. Not only that, it's likely that your headline will be unattractive to the people you brought in looking for a high quality widget (even if your product is high quality) because the main message you're saying immediately is that it's inexpensive.

You may look at this example and think it's just common sense, but it's astonishing how often businesses will drive traffic from ads to their main home page with no immediate continuity between the product/service the ad was for, instead of setting up a landing page that gives precisely the information the person was seeking (and matching what you claimed in your ad), without needing to make additional clicks or hunt around.

> **Techie Tip:** *The main headline should use an <H1> tag in the code so that search engines know that this is the main topic of the page.*

Secondary Headline – A secondary headline is not mandatory but it can be helpful. It's used to elaborate on the main headline or provide additional details. If you decide to use a secondary headline, it's important that there is cohesion and a relationship between the two.

Think of it like a newspaper article where there is a main headline, and underneath they have a sub headline that tells you more details about the story before actually getting into the story.

> **Techie Tip:** *A secondary headline should use an <H2> tag in the code so search engines know that, while this may not be the main point of the web page, it's more important than the other text.*

Value Proposition – The average page visit lasts a little less than a minute[1]. Therefore, you only have a few seconds to communicate your unique selling proposition (USP) or value proposition to the reader while building trust. To gain several minutes of user attention, you must clearly communicate your value proposition within 10 seconds[2].

In other words, a person who visits your landing page must clearly understand what benefit(s) your product or service will provide quickly and with minimal effort.

A value proposition answers why that specific prospect will choose your product or service over the competition. It addresses the on-going dialogue in your prospect's mind.

Title and URL – The title (the text that displays on the tab at the top of the web browser) and the URL of the page should be consistent with the headline.

---

[1] http://www.nngroup.com/articles/how-long-do-users-stay-on-web-pages/
[2] http://www.nngroup.com/articles/how-long-do-users-stay-on-web-pages/

Description – This is a section below the headline(s) that convinces the visitor you are talking to them and you can make their life better with your product/service. This can be done through text, video or some combination of the two.

At the end of the text or video, tell them what they need to do next (your goal) with a sense of urgency. Tell them to click the Buy It Now button or to complete the form to the right and hit Submit (to receive more information or a free gift) immediately. Take them by the hand and walk them through what to do.

> ***Techie Tip:*** *You may choose to add an image to supplement a text description. If an image is used, use the **"alt attribute."** The alt attribute is text that tells search engines what the image is about, since they can't "see" the image. It also provides additional context as to what the web page is about, so you want the alt attribute text to tie into the keywords for the page.*

Call To Action – Strong, clear verbiage is not the only thing that is important for the CTA. You want it to be very obvious on the page. It should also stick out visually, as to say, "Hey, you're supposed to click me!!!!" It's almost always best to associate the CTA with a button. When people see buttons, they associate it with action, and are more compelled to click it than a normal text link. This is not an Easter egg hunt – don't make people search for what to do next.

It might be tempting to have the button match the color scheme of your logo or the website of the business, but don't do it. Believe it or not, the color of a button has been tested over and over by Internet marketing experts and the best converting colors? Red and orange. While red or orange may not match your logo, they're commonly used because they promote action. Pay attention when you're surfing around the Internet or the next time you're making a purchase or responding to a CTA. Chances are, the button color is red or orange. Remember, the purpose of the button is not to look pretty, but to motivate people to proceed to the goal you defined.

Regardless of what you choose to use, make sure that you include button color when you conduct A/B testing of your landing page (read more about testing in the next section).

Not For The Faint Of Heart

To this point, the elements we talked about on a landing page are very important and need to have a fair amount of attention given to them. Make sure you take your time in putting together the proper, cohesive message. Map it all out before putting the elements in place to ensure continuity and likely conversion.

If you're not confident in your own verbal skills, then enlist the help of a trusted colleague or even hire a marketing or content professional who can help form the proper message. You can always take a cue from your existing marketing pieces (but only the ones that you know are effective in driving business) as a starting point, or check out what your competitors are doing.

Striving To Be Better

Creating a smart landing page is just the starting point for making your website work better for you. To ensure that you're getting the best results possible, continuously track how the page is doing and constantly tweak it based on the results you find.

In other words, you'll want to **optimize the page**. You want to make any necessary adjustments so that it performs as well as it possibly can.

You'll measure your success with your conversion rate - the percent of times that a visitor completes the goal you define. For example, if your goal is for someone to submit a web form giving you their contact information, your conversion rate would be how often a person does that from your landing page. If you have 100 visitors to the page and 13 submit their information, your conversion rate is 13%.

The challenge is to make your conversion rate as high as possible. To ensure this, do **A/B testing**. A/B testing is when you test one version of a page against another version that is basically the same, but has some sort of a modification. Usually one thing at a time is changed.

Some examples of modifications may be:
- Change of font size (for the headlines or body text)
- Change of font colors
- Different text (in the body or call to action)
- Different headline
- Change of image/video
- Change of button color
- Change of button size
- Change the location or placement of things (button, image/video, headline, form, etc.) on the page

This only a sampling of the changes you can test; you can really alter just about any element on your page and test it.

One thing to be cognizant of is to try and limit your changes to one thing at a time. If you make multiple changes and see a move in your conversion rate, you can't be entirely sure which change caused it unless you do one at a time.

To test the variation, simply divert some or all of your traffic to the modified landing page for a period of time. You just want enough traffic to reach the page so that it's an adequate sample size to determine which version converted better: A (the original) or B (the new version). Hence, the term, A/B testing.

Keep repeating this exercise with iterations until you have the conversion rate as high as you can get it. That's when your page is optimized.

But don't rest on your laurels for too long. Continue to closely monitor your analytics because landing pages have a shelf life.

Landing pages, like ads and just about all other aspects of the web, can get stale and ineffective for a variety of reasons. Essentially, they expire. Soon enough you'll find it's time to retire your landing page when it's no longer profitable for you and the conversion rate is dropping steadily. The content or offer may get outdated, the benefits are no longer attractive or people might just be sick of seeing the same thing over and over again.

When the analytics tell you that time has come, create a brand new landing page and start the process over again.

It's all about trusting the numbers.

The Challenge With CTAs

Many times it's unclear what the main CTA is for a web page. The problem may be that there is no clear CTA driving the visitor to the intended goal of a page.

How often have you been to the site of a service provider where they describe what they do, but don't have a form on that page for either scheduling an appointment or learning additional information? Yes, they have a link to Contact Us on the menu, but that's not the same. People can be lazy and impatient on the Internet so even if it's just one additional click, the chances of them contacting that service provider to schedule an appointment or ask questions drops significantly if the option is not made blatantly clear and simple.

While many pages lack a dominant CTA, the biggest reason most web pages don't convert as high as landing pages is because they have too many options for visitors. They are calling people to act on too many things.

Imagine walking down the street and you come to a sign that has ten different attractions listed with arrows pointing in different directions. If you just have the option of going to Attraction A, the chances would be higher that you would go there than if you had to pick between Attractions A-J.

Compare that to web pages where a visitor can click on a variety of links: About Us, Products/Services, ads, promotions, Blog, Contact Us, and external links. Aside from all those there's often an option to: add the company as a social networking friend, share the link of the page, comment/review, subscribe to a newsletter, or live chat. Each of these effectively are distractions and can decrease the chance that the main CTA (sale, lead) occurs.

Many of the elements just mentioned are not bad for most web pages – they can build trust with the potential customer. But if your goal is higher conversion rates and reaching your pre-determined goals, they end up being clutter.

Remember, here we're focusing on how a landing page differs from a typical web page and can produce higher conversion rates, which can positively impact your bottom line.

3: Resources

Clicktale (http://www.clicktale.com/) – A tool for recording website visits so you can watch a video and see where people are actually looking and clicking when they are at your website.

Google Analytics (http://google.com/analytics) – Provides statistics and data on website visitors and tells who is looking at the site, why they're visiting, how they're getting there, and how much profit you're making from them.

Google Analytics Gallery (https://www.google.com/analytics/gallery/) – A place where you can obtain additional Google Analytics reports (outside of the basic reports provided with your account) that people have created for free.

3: Actionable Checklist

- Have you set up Google Analytics for your site(s)?
- Are there any additional reports you found in the Google Analytics Gallery that would be useful for your business?
- Is it immediately clear what your value proposition is on your landing page(s)?
- Is your CTA very clear?
- Do you only have one CTA on your landing page?
- Are all the elements of your landing page cohesive?
- Have you identified elements of your page that you can use for A/B testing to optimize your site?

[4]

Using Landing Pages for Lead Generation

Now that we've decoded some of the secrets behind a successful landing page, let's look a little more closely at how to escort the visitor through the buying process.

By this point, they are becoming aware of you and your product. **Now you have to convince them that they need what you offer and must make the purchase.**

Purchases for big ticket items and services can take longer, largely because of the money people stand to lose and the question of whether they can trust you. The challenge with an online presence is that you have visitors who may be considering buying from or working with you and you don't even know it.

To make the sale, you need to capture their contact information so you can follow-up with them to address any lingering doubts and close the sale. This is where landing pages can help.

Landing pages are great tools for lead generation – they can produce much higher conversion rates than trying to get someone to communicate with you via a contact page if they're set-up right. Aside from being properly set up like we discussed in the last step, another thing you can do is **offer lead incentives that motivate visitors to provide their contact details in exchange for something you offer them.**

It's an ethical bribe.

With Lead Generation, Qualify For Higher Profitability

Your website often is the first touch point a prospect/client has with your company. It is your digital salesperson. Think about it, when you first learn about a company, where's the first place you go to find out more? You go online.

However, just like your top salesperson, your site must qualify the prospective customer to ensure you're a good fit for each other. And that qualification begins on a landing page. If you don't qualify prospects, you could end up wasting a lot of your time and losing profitability.

Not everyone who finds your landing page will be a good fit for your company. Some are unlikely buyers, while others are looking for something that you can't, or don't, offer.

There are two basic ways to qualify visitors: (1) ask the right questions in the web form on the landing page, and/or (2) describe who you're looking for in the description.

Is this prospect a potential good customer (a good fit for your company)?
- Can they afford your services?
- Can you help this prospect?
- Are they a likely buyer?
- Will they be too much of a "time suck" (take up more time than you'll regain in profit)?
- Will they cost more money than they bring in?
- Do you have what they are looking for?

One way to eliminate time sucks is by not only describing your product/service clearly, but by explaining who your target customer is. While you may be turning away some potential business (from less profitable customers), in the end, if you already know who your most profitable customers are, you can focus on attracting more just like them, thereby increasing profits.

If you're selling a big ticket product or a service and you don't want to show your price on your site, it's extra important to qualify people to prevent sticker shock. One way to do this is indicating who can typically afford your offerings.

Some examples:
- "Our services are not the cheapest, but you'll find us well worth our prices because…"
- "We offer our exclusive services to high net worth clients with $500,000 to invest."
- "Our typical clients include small businesses with over [xx] employees, with [$xxx] in annual revenue, etc."
- "We serve businesses in the [industry] who are looking to [goal]."

You can also incorporate certain questions in the web form of your landing page to see if a person is likely to buy from you. Why waste your time asking the prospect these questions later, when you can have the answer before you even pick up the phone or write an email?

If you're concerned whether someone can afford your services, consider asking:
- Annual household income (for individuals).
- Annual revenue (for business).
- Number of employees.

- How much they are thinking about spending for this service.

If you're interested in finding out how serious of a buyer they are, ask:
- When they plan to buy (i.e. immediately, next six months, next 12 months, etc.).
- How often they buy.
- Who they have bought from in the past.

Keep in mind, there is a strong negative correlation between conversion rates and the number of questions you ask and how personal they are. In other words, the more personal you get and the more questions you ask, the fewer the people who will fill out your web form. So ask a few targeted questions to qualify them (and weed out unlikely buyers), and stop there. You can reduce the number of questions later if your conversion rate is too low or add some if you're getting too many unqualified prospects.

REMEMBER: IT'S A PROCESS, NOT A SPRINT

With services or high-dollar products, the buying decision is often a process. The decision to make these purchases online is rarely done on impulse. Instead, people need additional time and information to make their final decision. In this regard, the online buying process is not much different than the offline process.

For expensive items, the person may need to shop around and determine if the large amount of money they are about to spend is really worth it, and find out what the viable options are (i.e. other sellers, different products). For services, which are harder to conceptualize online because you can't see pictures of it or return it (like a product), the person needs to be convinced that they need the service and you are the right business for the job. Somehow you have to gain their trust without meeting with them in person.

Keep in mind **attention, interest, desire, and action** (AIDA) from the previous step. A buyer will go through all of these phases before they make a purchase, even if they spend a shorter amount of time inside one component or another.

Understanding this cycle is critical for your business. For example, if you push the person for the sale before they've gone through the interest or desire stage, they likely won't buy. They will not be convinced that they need the service/product or that you're the one they should buy from.

Your landing page should start the process by creating an awareness of your product/service and then offer them a lead incentive, something that entices them to provide their contact information and aids their research.

Typical items to offer in exchange for filling out a web form on the landing page (an ethical bribe) can include:
- Registration for a webinar

- A downloadable white paper or eBook
- A phone call
- A special video
- A free trial offer

These incentives should help alleviate concerns that the person has about buying from you and emphasize the benefits of what they will receive for their money.

You can greatly enhance the conversion rate of visitors turning into customers by: (1) ensuring that your lead generation form is connected to an autoresponder and (2) personally following up on leads.

Email services like AWeber and MailChimp offer functionality called **autoresponders** which automatically send emails to people who fill out forms according to a predetermined schedule. You probably receive any number of autoresponders throughout the day. For example, when a person fills out the form on your site, they receive an email with the white paper you promised on your landing page (your offer), and then they will receive subsequent emails on a set schedule, say 3, 7 and 10 days after their initial sign-up they get a new email – each one unique and addressing a different concern or benefit.

Hopefully, after receiving these emails, the person either buys from you or contacts you. Even if they don't, you can still gauge their interest by reviewing the email statistics (which you have access to with services like AWeber and MailChimp) to see how often they opened your emails to read them. Email services provide analytics and reporting options just like we saw earlier with Google Analytics. They will tell you how many people received your email, how many opened it, how many read it, how many clicked on the links, etc.

Aside from using an autoresponder, personally follow-up with your leads (autoresponder does not mean autopilot). The more individualized you're able to make that follow up, the better. Ideally you will call each qualified lead that you have. To increase the chance that you're calling likely buyers, you may decide to only call people that read a certain email. In these cases, it can be an easier conversation because you can then explain how you noticed they signed up to receive your offer and that they read the email, and you're calling to find out if they had any questions.

The Top 5 Types of Lead Incentives

What makes a good bribe (we'll call it a **lead incentive**) for motivating people to give their contact information on a landing page? **It is one that provides value.**

The lead incentive should be enticing enough that someone is willing to give up their contact information to get it.

It should be something that they need. This could be something like a free trial, product or service, but it also could be some information or education that they are curious about.

A lead incentive demonstrates expertise. It should prove why you are the business to buy from. It shows that you are an expert on this subject matter or that you produce quality products. Basically, it builds up your credibility and the amount of trust that the prospective buyer has in you.

It leads to a buying decision. Before people buy they need to feel like they have enough information to make their decision. They need to understand:
- What are the benefits of the product/service?
- What are the risks of buying it?
- Is it worth the cost (money, time, effort, etc.)?
- Is now the time to buy it?
- Who is the best to buy from?

Your lead incentive must answer these questions to motivate the prospect to buy from you. If it does, you will help them make their buying decision. Provide them with the answers they need and build trust, and you have a great shot at making the sale.

(1) White Paper or eBook

White papers or eBooks are 5-7 page PDFs that gives quality information related to the product or service you're selling. An effective white paper or eBook piques the person's interest by answering a question that they feel like they need to know the answer to. Here are some examples of white paper or eBook titles:

If you're selling...
- Veterinarian Services => **How To Select A Veterinarian**
- Beans/Legumes => **Improve Your Health With A High Fiber Diet**
- CPA Services => **How To Avoid IRS Audits**
- Law Services => **The Seven Biggest Risks To Start-Up Businesses**
- Yachts => **What You Need to Know Before Buying A Boat**

The white paper or eBook should help them make a buying decision by countering any doubts that they may have about the purchase. It should contain enough information to demonstrate your knowledge so you are seen as an expert.

If you're not confident in putting together your own white paper or ebook, you can hire a freelance writing professional to help put your words and ideas into a cohesive finished product. In the next step we're going to talk more about content and how to source some great content to use on your site.

Also, since your content will be great, make sure your finished product looks professional and is branded for your company. Don't worry if you're not artistic, you can hire someone to spruce up your PDF for an affordable price by using freelance sites.

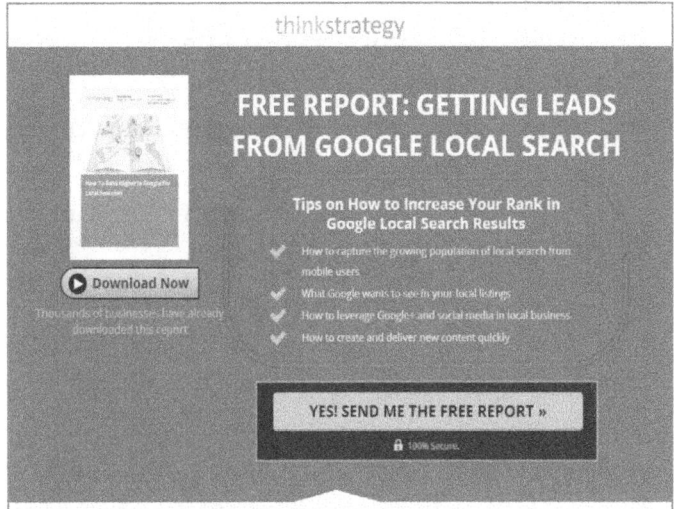

(2) Case Studies

Case studies are examples featuring existing clients that faced similar issues or problems that the prospective customer has, followed by the solution that you provided and the final results. Position it as valuable by providing testimonials – quotes from others who found the material beneficial – right on the landing page.

The case studies should demonstrate your knowledge and successful track record to build confidence that you're the business to buy from. It should also focus on painting the vision of how the customer's life will improve once they buy your product or service.

If you're selling...

- A Weight Loss Product => **Learn How Steve Lost 10 Pounds In A Month**
- Tutoring Services => **How Our System Turned Students From Failing To Straight A's**
- Safety Products => **How We Reduced The Number Of Workplace Incidents By 40%**

Your case studies will come together from a real life example. You're not creating a story from thin air or from scratch; you're sharing an actual customer story. You'll include their problem or issue and then explain how your product or service solved the problem or addressed the issue. It almost writes itself.

Case studies can be written or presented via video.

(3) Event Registration

Sometimes you may find that publications are not effective at encouraging people to buy your product/service. This can be especially true if the product/service is complex, expensive and/or visual. In these cases, events may be the best way to drive sales.

Common types of events for prospects include:
- Seminars
- Webinars
- Open houses
- Product demonstrations

Seminars are informational sessions where a presentation is done to explain what your product/service does, how it will benefit the person, why they should buy from you, and alleviate any concerns they may have (through the materials provided and by allocating time for questions and answers). Seminars allow you to close sales in person, and give you an additional chance to build trust by meeting prospects face-to-face.

The downside is that they can be costly to conduct, depending on the venue (i.e. if you need to rent a space) and if there are materials you want to hand out. Also, it does take a time commitment, whereas a publication is something that a person can read on their own time.

Webinars are like seminars, only they are done over the Internet, where presenters can share their computer screen and talk to attendees using web apps. Webinars are increasingly being used by businesses because they are cheaper to put on than seminars and are more convenient for attendees. Webinars are also good for people who are visual because you can show things right on your computer screen.

Open houses are designated times where you welcome prospective customers to visit you at your business to learn more about your offerings. Typically they're a lot more informational than webinars and seminars.

Product demos let people see how products work; see them in action. Demos can be done online or in person. Many products don't sell well unless people can actually see how they work and how easy they are to use. A demo lends itself to selling more effectively to buyers who are visual learners, as opposed to readers.

Landing pages for any of these events should include a form for people to register. The easier it is for people to register for the event, the more likely they are to do so. After they register, you not only want to send an automated email to verify they registered, but then send reminders as the event approaches to reduce the amount of no-shows (one week before, the day before, the day of).

(4) Sample/Trial

If possible, you might consider offering a free sample or trial of your product/service so people can experience the benefits firsthand. Being able to use it increases confidence in your product/service and alleviates fears of risks that could be associated with the purchase.

A sample or trial can be a...
- 30-day supply of a product
- Limited trial version (so a person can experience, some, but maybe not all, of the benefits)
- Free product, with the person only paying shipping and handling
- Free services for one month (or a certain amount of time)

With a sample or trial you want to ensure they have enough time or product to realize the benefits, but you don't want to give away too much. If you do, they may not make the purchase because they have already gotten everything they need from the free trial.

(5) Coupons / Discounts

Coupons, discounts and promotion codes are another way to drive people to share their contact information. These are a good way to reduce the risk of the purchase to the potential customer (since they will pay less money), which encourages them to buy.

The downside to coupons or discounts is that you'll be cutting into your profit margin by receiving less money. Also, be cognizant of the fact that if you use a promotional code that provides a discount on your website, it may be shared via sites like RetailMeNot (http://retailmenot.com). The same is true if you provide a coupon the person can print from home – they may share it with others.

Hopefully now you see how valuable a properly built landing page is for lead generation, and how that process can help to get prospective customers knocking on your door.

You should also have some ideas now of the type of lead generation tool you can offer visitors to your site to begin the engagement process, based on your business.

Make sure you're jotting down notes as you go through these pages to add to your own master selling plan – you don't want to forget that million dollar idea!

4: Resources

Landing Pages

LeadPages (http://blog.leadpages.net/the-ultimate-list-of-free-landing-page-templates/) – Provides free landing page templates that you can customize and use as part of your website.

Graphic Design

99designs (http://99designs.com) – This site uses contests where graphic designers compete for projects. You describe what you want created and designers submit their ideas. If you find one that you like, you pay the winner a fixed amount that is listed on the site (which you can see before starting the contest). You don't pay if there aren't any submissions that you like.

Fiverr (http://fiverr.com) – On this site, people will do tasks for you for $5. You can hire people to do layouts and designs starting at only $5.

Email Marketing

AWeber (http://aweber.com) – Email software for creating lists of subscribers, setting up autoresponders and emailing to your list.

MailChimp (http://mailchimp.com) – Another email software option to create lists of subscribers, set-up autoresponders and email to your list.

Webinar/Presentation Software

GoToWebinar (http://www.gotomeeting.com/online/webinar/) – Pay a monthly fee to conduct webinars with your prospects. Offers self-service registration (for attendees), automated reminder emails (so people don't forget to attend), video conferencing, screen sharing, audio, and recording. Participants are given a link by which they join the webinar online.

Join.Me (http://join.me) – A free alternative to GoToWebiner that offers screen sharing and audio options. Although the functionality is not as robust as GoToWebinar, you are limited to having only ten participants and can't schedule meetings in the future with the free plan (you have to give the link to participants in real-time). This is a great option for on-the-fly webinars.

4: Actionable Checklist

- Have you properly qualified prospects (on landing pages for leads)?
- What are the biggest objections and/or fears your prospects have about buying?
- What are the main pain points you're trying to fix for your prospects?
- What kind of information would your customers love to have?
- What kind of lead incentives can you create that will alleviate customer fears, address at least one major pain point and be centered around a topic they want to know about?

[5]
Content is King

Now that we've looked at the base structure of your website, it's time to beef things up a little, and that's done with your content.

Content is king on the Internet. Period.

Content is what keeps people returning to your website. Content encourages engagement – actions and conversations – with your clients and prospective clients. Content is what people link to (and links generate traffic). Content is an integral part of the fiber of your website structure.

Not just any content though – good content.

Good content is:
- Relevant to your audience
- Unique
- Provides enough detail for your audience to act on

Thinking of good content takes time and can be frustrating, so we've created this list of ideas you can use whenever you need to develop content.

Constantly creating content is an important part of your website's success, not only because it entices people to keep coming back, but also because search engines like sites that provide fresh content. When search engines like Google realize that you are consistently creating content, they're more apt to send you traffic because it means that the information is more likely to be relevant since it's being updated (as opposed to a static site that rarely changes).

Before you go putting a lot of pressure on yourself to publish new stuff all the time, let's look at some ways and places to find great content. As with anything else, developing a strategy will help put the pieces in place and sketch out a timeline for regular postings.

Where to Get Ideas

Industry News Feeds

Stay on top of industry news with the least amount of effort and time by using RSS feeds and news aggregator apps. These free tools automatically receive news from industry media outlets so you can keep tabs on hot topics. Subscribe to news sources that are relevant to your industry and regularly flip through headlines to generate topic ideas.

There are many different news aggregator tools and sites out there, but one we really like is Feedly. **Feedly** is a great tool that allows you to subscribe to news feeds from websites, and setting it up is simple. As with many online tools, you'll want to set up an account to make the most use of the features.

(1) Once you log in to Feedly, click the *Add Content* link:

(2) On the next page, enter a topic or a website from which you want to get news:

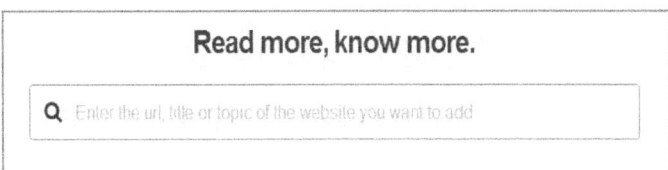

(3) On the Results page, you are shown suggestions and can choose to add a feed to your Feedly.

(4) After you add a news source to your Feedly, you'll see headlines in your feed as new articles are published. You can quickly glance at them and select any that you are interested in.

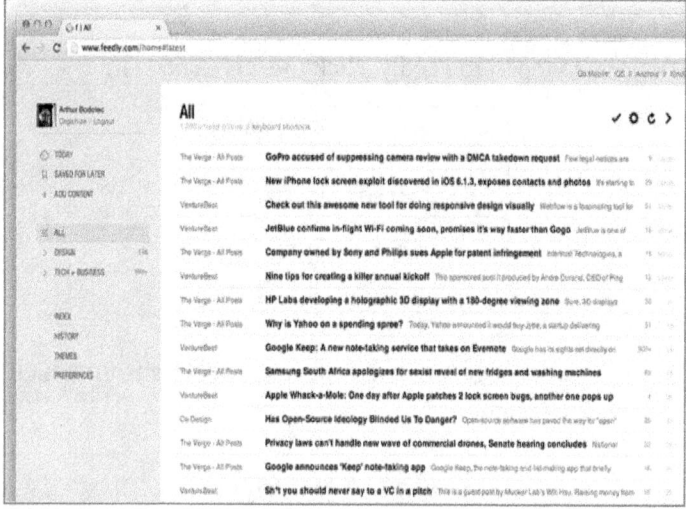

If you'd rather see the top news stories on the go, Flipboard is a popular smartphone and tablet app that works similarly to Feedly.

You can add news sources or topics and you will see articles after they are published. **Flipboard** is much more visually appealing than Feedly because they use images to accompany the articles, but it can also be more time consuming because they don't have a single view where you can see all of the headlines – you need to "flip" through to see all of the news. The reason for this is because Flipboard makes its money by showing ads as you flip through the articles (Feedly makes its money by offering premium features to users).

Sharing news with customers and prospects helps establish you as an industry leader who is on top of everything that's going on. It also builds confidence that you have a wide range of knowledge and that you have the ability to offer the best to visitors (because you're aware of the greatest).

Customer Questions

Use customer questions as a source for content ideas. As questions come in to either customer service or via email, collect all those questions and answers into one place and use them as new content.

There are two major benefits of using customer questions as a source: (1) you're addressing a topic that you know your customers are interested in and (2) you're preemptively answering a question that you know others have. That means you'll save time because you can point others that have the same question to this content, and you'll get additional traffic from others visitors who are prospective customers.

Social Networking Comments & Questions

Social networking is another way of listening to what your clients and prospects are interested in. Later in the book we'll focus on your business' social network presence and how to capitalize on it, but for now, understand what a valuable resource the networks can be for content.

Read any comments and questions, in addition to what they post, to gauge the type of content prospects or customers find valuable.

If you aren't getting anything useful, start the conversation with your audience by asking them what they would find valuable.

Ask:

- What would they like advice on?
- What are their biggest concerns about a product or service?
- What topics are they most interested in?
- Pose a question and see the responses (What do you think about ___? How do you feel about ___?).

Competitor Sites

Check your competitors' blogs, press releases and social media accounts regularly to keep tabs on the content that they are sharing with their customers and fans. It can show you not only content ideas, but also their marketing strategy – who they're targeting, products/services that they think are opportunities and industry trends that they are seeing.

Your Own Popular Content

Use your analytics to see what your most popular content is – what's been visited the most, what has the most comments, what has been downloaded the most, etc. This will give you an indication of related topics you might write about. In fact, you may continue to write on one topic but expand on it, turning it into a series.

To find out what the most popular content on your site is, turn to your Google Analytics reports that we talked about in Step 3.

In Google Analytics, a few reports you may use to find out what's popular are:

Site Content - All Pages (in the left menu, go to: Behavior > Site Content > All Pages) – This report will tell you what your most popular pages are and which ones visitors are spending the most time on.

Page	Pageviews	Unique Pageviews	Avg. Time on Page
	1,102 % of Total: 100.00% (1,102)	822 % of Total: 100.00% (822)	00:02:07 Site Avg: 00:02:07 (0.00%)
1. /	320 (29.04%)	224 (27.25%)	00:03:31
2. /how-to-competitive-analysis/	99 (8.98%)	75 (9.12%)	00:01:41
3. /about-us/	50 (4.54%)	36 (4.38%)	00:02:00
4. /think-traffic/	45 (4.08%)	21 (2.55%)	00:01:15
5. /contact/	36 (3.27%)	32 (3.89%)	00:03:09
6. /finding-hot-product-trends/	36 (3.27%)	28 (3.41%)	00:07:14
7. /blog/	35 (3.18%)	29 (3.53%)	00:00:50
8. /services/	26 (2.36%)	20 (2.43%)	00:01:47
9. /portfolio/	24 (2.18%)	22 (2.68%)	00:00:17
10. /free-web-consultation/	21 (1.91%)	12 (1.46%)	00:01:27

Search Engine Optimization - Queries (in the left menu, go to: Acquisition > Search Engine Optimization > Queries) – This report will tell you which web searches you show up in, how popular those searches are and how often people are clicking on your site from the given search results.

Query	Impressions	Clicks	Average Position	CTR
	819 % of Total: 51.19% (1,600)	41 % of Total: 117.14% (35)	63 Site Avg. 120 (-46.37%)	5.01% Site Avg: 2.19% (128.85%)
1. how to get more followers on instagram	110 (13.43%)	0 (0.00%)	130	0.00%
2. sales funnel management	110 (13.43%)	0 (0.00%)	52	0.00%
3. think strategy	70 (8.55%)	16 (39.02%)	26	22.86%
4. how to get more instagram followers	60 (7.33%)	0 (0.00%)	110	0.00%
5. funnelmanagement	50 (6.11%)	0 (0.00%)	33	0.00%
6. seo funnel	35 (4.27%)	0 (0.00%)	58	0.00%
7. generate website traffic	22 (2.69%)	0 (0.00%)	120	0.00%
8. get more instagram followers free	22 (2.69%)	0 (0.00%)	160	0.00%
9. sem strategy	22 (2.69%)	0 (0.00%)	87	0.00%
10. how do facebook ads work	16 (1.95%)	0 (0.00%)	65	0.00%

Search Engine Autocomplete - To make finding things on the Internet easier, search engines such as Google and Bing suggest things to search for based on what you type into the Search box.

The suggestions, referred to as autocomplete, are based on popular searches. For example, when you go to Bing and type "how to account" (which might lead to a good topic for an accounting, finance or bookkeeping business) these suggestions are provided:

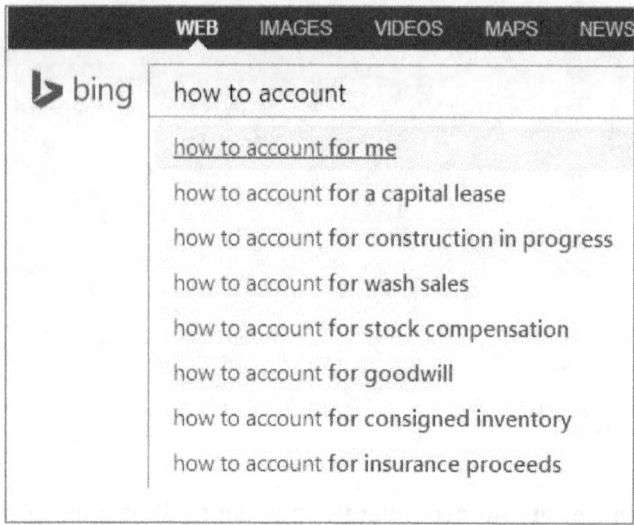

This is a very powerful strategy because it means that people are already looking for these topics, so if you create related content, when people search for this in the future, they can be directed to your site.

Reddit

Reddit is a popular website that allows people to submit and vote on articles that they find valuable. To find topics that people are interested in, search for keywords for your industry – words related to your services/products or ones around topics your customers might be interested in.

For example, if you were to look up "marketing," here are the most popular articles (below). Reddit then gives you the option to filter the list so you can zero in on something more relevant, if need be.

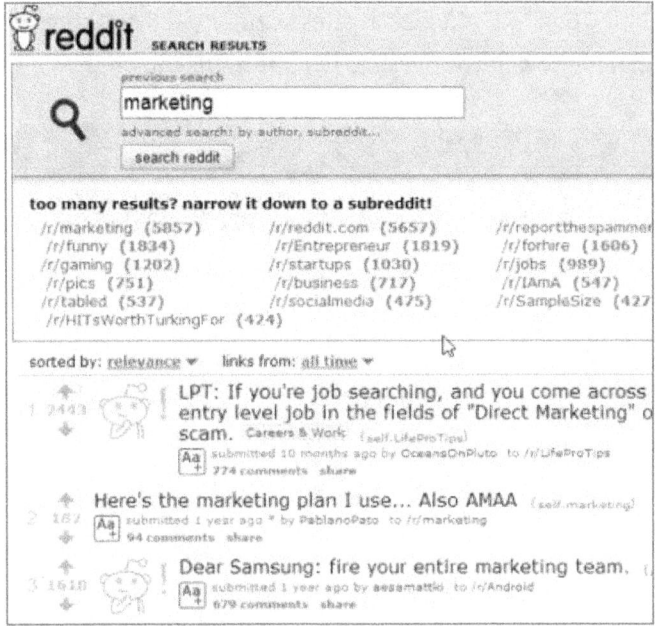

StumbleUpon a Topic

Similar to Reddit, StumbleUpon is a social networking site that lets users submit sites and then vote on them. It works a little differently than Reddit though.

Reddit allows you to see lists of the most popular articles, whereas StumbleUpon forces you to "stumble," or click through them via a toolbar at the top of your Internet browser window. They'll show you a site, and you have the option to skip to the next one by clicking the "Stumble" button.

StumbleUpon lets you look at sites segmented by interest so you can narrow down the sites to your industry.

SlideShare And YouTube

SlideShare and YouTube are great content sites that will tell you how popular certain topics are. You can do searches on subjects related to your industry and see the number of page views a video receives to gauge your interest.

If You Answer It, They Will Come

Quora and Yahoo Answers can be used to see what questions are on the minds of people. Take the questions that people post as topic ideas for your content. As a side benefit, if you register for the sites, you can answer a question and provide a link to your content to drive traffic back to your site.

For example, a search for "aquarium" shows some questions that would help businesses that:
- Sell fish tanks
- Clean fish tanks

- Sell pet fish
- Sell pet supplies

By answering questions, you can prove that you're an expert in an area for that person and all future readers (who likely have the same concern).

What's Trending Now?

Google Trends is a great place to learn about topics that are currently trending online. There are a host of ways you can cull through the data, including Hot Searches, Correlate Searches, Top Charts, and more.

While you may not find something specific that you can use every day, you may find ways to correlate information or tie topics together, thereby capitalizing on the popular topics at the time.

While we're talking about Google, we can't forget about Google Insights, which is another way to identify hot or trending topics.

The tools we mention here are just the tip of the iceberg. There are new sites and tools coming online everyday, especially with the popularity of content curation – there is a huge interest in finding and providing quality content online, and the advantage for us is that it's never been easier to find something to talk about.

Speaking of what to talk about, let's go there next.

What To Talk About

Now that you have an idea of subjects or broad topics that might be of interest to your target market, you have to figure out what to write about.

Keep in mind that content can be video as well as text. In fact, video is probably the way to go in many cases, if possible, since it is more personable and generally converts better than copy.

What are some of the most popular and easiest types of content to talk about?

How-To's

Create a how-to article or video related to a particular subject.
- How to shop for something (criteria or factors people should look at when deciding who to buy from).
- How to do a certain aspect of a service you provide.

Lists

Lists are extremely popular on the Internet – maybe because they are perceived to be quick reads that answer questions fast.
- The 5 Best...
- 26 Ways To...
- 7 Reasons Why...
- 11 Things You Can Learn From...

Interviews

Interview subject matter experts to talk about something. The interviews could be done with someone from your business or outside of your business who has a unique or useful perspective on something related to what you do.

If it's not someone from your business, it could boost the credibility of your content because people will be more inclined to believe that the information is from a neutral third party.

Interviews can be presented as video, text or both (i.e. video with a written transcript of the text). It can be a question and answer type format or the interviewee simply talking about the subject. The interview doesn't have to be formal and scripted, it can just be a conversation that flows either along some feeder questions or completely off-the-cuff.

Impact Of Recent News

Put your own spin on industry news by talking about what the news is and then going into detail about how this news impacts your target market. Also, let them know what they can do to either take advantage of the information or how they can protect themselves.

The Answer Post

Take questions that your target market or customers have and answer them. Simple. We alluded to this earlier when we talked about compiling your customer service questions.

One thing to consider when you're doing this is, you may want to make the title of the webpage the subject of the question you are answering. For example, if your question is, "How Do I File A Cease And Desist Order?" make that the title of the page. It will tell your current customers, fans and followers immediately what pain point you're addressing. It will also help your content in search rankings because there are most likely people searching for the answer to that question (and there are not a lot of pages with that title) which tells search engines it is very relevant for certain searches.

The Repurpose

Sometimes you'll find content on another site (or multiple sites) that you can tweak slightly and "make it your own" to produce something new for your site. You can use the original content as a baseline, and then adjust the wording to make it your own or to put your own spin on it. If you're taking content from many different places and bringing it together in one place, you're **curating** content. Think of it like a curator in a museum. A curator gathers relevant works from many different sources and presents them together in a new and interesting way. That's exactly what you're doing here, but with content.

You can also change the media (format) to repurpose something. For example, if the original content was in text, maybe you make a video, presentation/slide show or white paper on the same topic.

Curating content can take effort and time, but it can be well worth it. In the long run, the objective of Google, Bing and Facebook is to promote content that people find valuable. There are far too many sites that produce content that didn't require much thought, but doesn't add value. Make meaningful content and you'll be rewarded with traffic.

5: Resources

Industry News Feeds/Trends

Feedly (http://feedly.com) – An app (web and mobile) that allows you subscribe to news sources and receive links to stories as they post. You can view the headlines to all of the stories you haven't read in one list and scroll through it quickly to see what interests you.

Flipboard (http://flipboard.com) – A mobile app that lets you subscribe to news sources and topics and see links to the stories. Flipboard is more visual than Feedly, which makes it more aesthetically pleasing, but it also takes more time to flip through all of the stories (no consolidated view of all of the headlines).

Google Trends (http://www.google.com/trends) - This is a great source to learn about the current topics that are trending online. You can run Hot Searches, Correlates and see Top Charts. Pairs well with Google Insights.

Question & Answer

Quora (http://quora.com) – A question and answer site where you can show your expertise by responding to people's queries and learn about topics that may be on the minds of your target market. Subscribe to topics to receive an email every time someone asks a question that you may know the answer to.

Yahoo Answers (https://www.answers.yahoo.com/) – Another free question and answer site to demonstrate your knowledge. You can't subscribe to topics like Quora, so you have to try to regularly look for questions you can answer.

Social Media Sites

Reddit (http://reddit.com) – A content sharing site where users vote for good articles. A great tool for learning about subjects that people may be interested in reading about on your site.

SlideShare (http://slideshare.com) – A site to share presentations (i.e. PowerPoint). By searching for keywords related to your business, you can see which subjects people are most interested in by noting which presentations get the most views.

StumbleUpon (http://stumbleupon.com) – Stumble through content on this social site to see what content that people submit receives the most "Up" votes.

YouTube (http://youtube.com) – This most popular video site can tell you what people are interested in, if you search on keywords related to your business. You may also thumb through the comments to see what particular aspects of the content people liked or where they found it lacking.

5: Actionable Checklist

- Could you use more industry news so that you have a constant funnel of information/content to share with potential customers?
- Which industry websites are going to be the most lucrative for mining information for your business?
- Have you tried using search engines to see what people are looking for?
- Have you tried using Reddit and StumbleUpon to see which topics are popular?
- Have you searched YouTube for popular content?
- Have you checked competitors' sites and social media profiles to see what content they're offering?
- Have you researched questions people have on different Q&A websites?
- Have you checked Google Trends and Google Insights for any recent news related to your business?
- Have you analyzed your own existing content or customer service database to find topics to discuss?
- Can you identify any industry experts that would be great candidates for an interview?

Part Two

Using SEO to Generate Free Traffic

[6]

Setting Up Your Technical Infrastructure for SEO

Now that you've created a solid foundation for your website, it is time to get some traffic.

The first thing you want to focus on is **search engine optimization (SEO)** to ensure that you are ranking as high as you can in Google, Bing and Yahoo (showing up on one of the first pages of search results, and as close to the top of the page as possible).

With search engines, there are two types of traffic, paid and organic. Paid traffic is just that – you're paying money to place ads to encourage visits to your website. Organic traffic is traffic that occurs from people finding you in search results.

Organic traffic can cost significantly less money than paid advertising over time because you don't have to pay based on volume. With online advertising, you typically pay based on how many people click on your ad or see your ad **(pay per click, or PPC).** With traffic resulting from people clicking on search results (organic), you don't pay for each visitor who clicks to visit your site or from them seeing your search result.

Some businesses will pay to have someone else handle SEO-related tasks for them. There are many great marketers out there who specialize in SEO and traffic generation and in some cases, that cost is minimal compared to the resulting traffic and profit. But for many business owners, outsourcing SEO management is not an option.

So what we want to do here is give you some information and tips on what to do right now to start driving traffic and increasing your SEO by yourself.

Double Vision?

We need to start the SEO discussion with one fundamental issue. While you may think that you have only one website, search engines may think that you have two. Try a simple test to find out:

(1) Type [yoursite].com in the browser address bar, and then click enter:

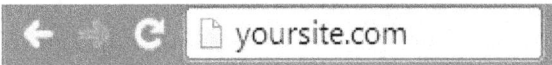

(2) Once the site loads, record the URL that is now in the address bar – most likely it will be [yoursite].com or www.[yoursite].com.

(3) Now, type www.[yoursite].com in the browser address bar, and then click enter.

(4) Compare that to the address you recorded in step 2.

Are they the same? If they are, you're OK and have just one site.

If not, search engines are seeing your website as two different ones. To fix this, you need to set-up a **301 redirect** with your web host after you decide what site you want people to use, www.[yoursite].com or [yoursite].com (without the www.). It doesn't matter too much which one you choose, and setting up a 301 redirect isn't as complicated as it sounds. If you're not the one managing your site, make sure you ask the appropriate person to do this change for you.

Once you decide which one you want to use, log into your website host's settings. Each host has their own way of doing things, but in general, there should be an area that allows you to set up redirects. You'll want to set-up something like the examples below. These tell the server that if someone types in http://thinkstrategy.com, they should be sent to http://www.thinkstrategy.com instead.

Domain	Directory	Redirect Url	Type
thewebsitelie.com	/	http://www.thewebsitelie.com/	permanent
thinkstrategy.com	/	http://www.thinkstrategy.com/	permanent

This way, whenever a search engine "crawls" or scans your site, they always record each page as one page.

If the redirect in this example were not set-up, the search engines would record thinkstrategy.com/example and www.thinkstrategy.com/example as two different pages. **The problem with that is those two pages (even though they have the same content) are now competing against each other for rankings in search results, which makes each one individually rank lower.** Not only that, but Google may view it as duplicate content, further hurting the rank of that content (duplicate content is interpreted as not beneficial to people, so Google often penalizes something it thinks is redundant because it adds limited value).

Help Me Help You

Now, once the search engine can find your one and only site (you've eliminated any harmful duplicates), it's time to show it what you've got.

Search engines can crawl your site looking for pages using links or you could just tell Google and Bing what you have on your site. However, if Google and Bing are going to help you get traffic by showing links to your site in their search results, why not make it easy for them?

Tell the search engines what pages are on your site and when you create or modify one. You can do this with a **sitemap**.

Software to create websites often includes functionality that creates and maintains sitemaps automatically. For example, Wordpress offers plugins that create them. These are free and not only manage your sitemap, but alert the search engines whenever you make a change to your site.

If you don't use software that includes this functionality, there are free tools you can use to manually create sitemaps. They require a little more work because you have to specifically use this tool whenever you want an update to show up for the search engines (i.e. pages created or added). You also have to upload the new file to your server. However, this small bit of extra work is worth it if you want traffic from search results.

Be The [Web] Master Of Your Domain

Since you already have your Google Analytics code installed and working on your website, you can sign up for a **Google**

Webmaster Tools account – this is how you tell Google that you have a sitemap and where it can be found. To let Google know about your sitemap, in your Webmaster Tools account:

(1) Using the left navigation menu, go to *Crawl > Sitemaps*

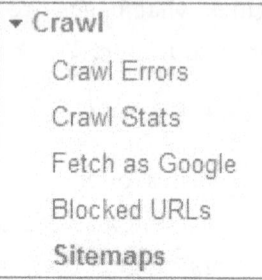

(2) Click the button for *Add/Test Sitemap*

(3) In the pop-up box, enter the location of the Sitemap on your server. If your website software automatically creates the sitemap, it should let you know where it places the file. The most common place is *yoursite.com/sitemap.xml* or *your-*

site.com/sitemap_index.xml. Click Submit Sitemap.

To activate **Bing Webmaster Tools** (and let it know where your sitemap is), visit their site, sign up for an account and then verify that you own the site. There are a number of ways to do that. You can upload a small file to your server, add a record to your domain settings or add a meta tag (small line of code) to your site. The process is simple and can be verified as soon as you add the code or make the setting change. Don't worry, if you're not familiar with code, verify you own the website by making changes with your domain registrar (GoDaddy, Register.com, etc.) because their instructions are pretty straightforward.

To let Bing know about your sitemap:

(1) Use the left navigation menu, go to Configure *My Site > Sitemaps*.

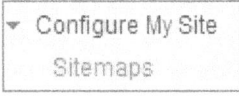

(2) On the Sitemaps page, enter the URL where your Sitemap is located, and then click *Submit*.

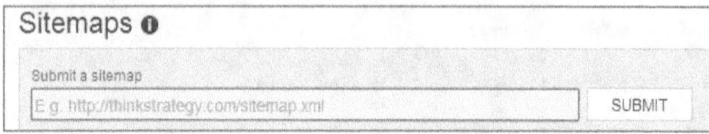

It's that easy.

Once you're set up in the search engines, you'll soon learn what Google and Bing think of your site and any problems they run into. Here's a sampling of their reporting:

Google
Crawl Errors (*Crawl > Crawl Errors*)

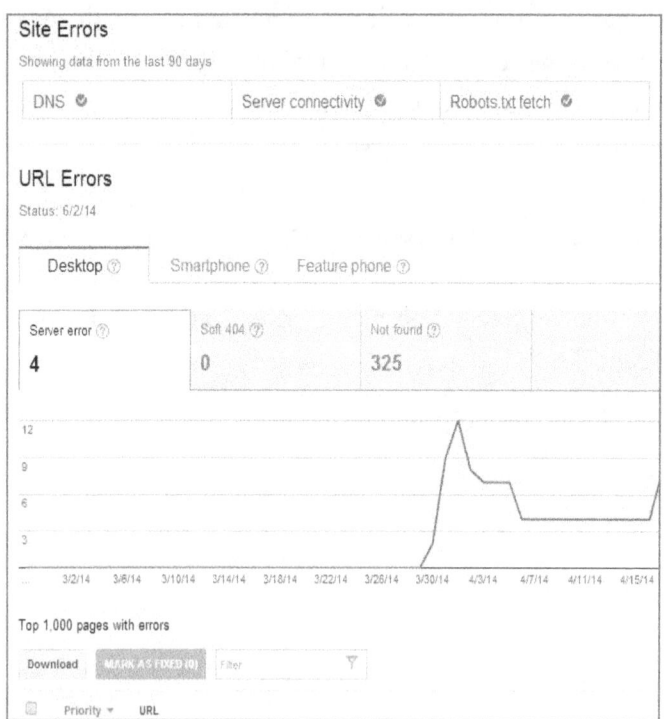

Sitemaps (*Crawl > Sitemaps*)

Bing

Crawl Information (*Reports & Data > Crawl Information*)

When you get the reports, take note of any issues the crawlers found. Each search engine will have a guide to walk you through how to interpret the reports. If you're web savvy, immediately tend to any problems that showed up. If you're not managing your own site, forward the reports to your web master for correction.

Need For Speed

Google wants its users to have the best user experience possible. This not only includes finding the sites that are most relevant to the keywords that person searches for, but also guiding them to sites that provide things like fresh content, a responsive design and ones that load relatively quickly. We've already discussed keeping your content fresh and ensuring that your site functions well on mobile devices and desktops (is responsive).

Now it's time to talk speed.

We've all been there – getting to a website that takes so long to load that we get frustrated and end up leaving. While your site (hopefully) may not be that slow, you can still work to make it perform as fast as possible.

Your choice of web host greatly impacts the performance of your site (with hosting on shared servers generally being the cheapest, but slowest), however that's only the start of the story.

You can tell how fast your site is and learn some ways to speed it up using free tools on the Internet.

Mini(mize) Me
You can increase the speed that your web page loads by reducing the resources required for a browser to pull up your page.

Huh?

Another way to say that it is making it easier and faster to load your page. The biggest culprits that slow down your page load time (resource hogs) are too many JavaScript and CSS files and large files.

Most web pages use JavaScript and Cascading Style Sheets (CSS) files somewhere in their DNA. JavaScript provides functionality for the site, such as changing how a button looks when you hover a cursor over it. CSS files help tell the browser how your web page should look – what colors to use, font styles and sizes, etc. The issue is that there are often multiple JavaScript and CSS files on one page, and each one needs time to load. Of course, the more files there are to load, the more time it takes to render (show) the web page. Therefore, to reduce the load time, you want to "minify" them.

Minification reduces page load speed by combining all JavaScript files into one and merging the CSS files. Loading one JavaScript and one CSS means that the browser doesn't need to wait for 5-20 files to load – only two. That can make a significant difference in how fast someone gets to see your whole page, and can mean the difference between their staying to learn more or leaving to find your competitor.

There are tools available to help you combine the files if you aren't a web developer.

One word of caution is that before you do this, make sure that you save a copy of your current website set-up just in case something goes wrong. Do a backup. Sometimes, when you combine files, it could cause errors if things load in the wrong order. If you have a backup, you can save what you lost and not have to rebuild from scratch.

Another thing that you can do is minimize the file size of images. Image files can often be reduced in size – memory-wise – without losing much quality (if any). Decreasing the file size results in less for the browser to download. If you're using Wordpress for your website, there are plugins that automatically compress the size of the image when you upload one. For non-Wordpress sites, there are free web apps you can use to reduce the size of images before you upload them to your site.

Caching

Caching speeds up your site by allowing your web page to appear (load) without involving your server. What happens is that you either code your website or use a tool to tell browsers that this web page usually only changes after a specified amount of time. Once a browser knows that, it will look to reuse copies of the files that it already downloaded to render the page. It basically saves it and brings it back up the next time you go to that site.

For example, let's say that you are using caching and have specified that the browser can expect that this page is typically good for a day; it won't change more frequently than that. If Dave visits yoursite.com after being there earlier in the day, the web page will load from the local cache instead downloading from the server. In other words, whenever you visit a website, it stores temporary files on your computer and if you visit again (caching is enabled) your browser will load files and data from there instead of from the server.

This saves time in two respects: (1) the data doesn't need to be sent across the Internet, and (2) the server doesn't need to process the request (interpret what data is needed and send it back).

Bring The Data Closer
Caching is not effective unless there is a copy of the web page stored somewhere other than your server. It works when a visitor goes to the page more than once, but that

means that the first time they load it, it will still have to talk to the server.

Here's where Content Delivery Networks (CDNs) help.
CDNs are networks of servers that are geographically dispersed and hold a cached version of your site. There are a couple of benefits that allow them to greatly help your page load speed: (1) they hold caches, so even if the visitor never visited your site they are still getting the page without waiting for a server to process, and (2) the geographic dispersion cuts down the physical distance the data has to travel – it will automatically load from the server that is closest to them.

Depending on the CDN, some offer additional functionality such as minifying files for you, spam protection and security against some hacking attacks.

Rich Snippets
Depending on the type of content that your site has, you might think about integrating code for rich snippets as a way to improve your search rankings. Rich snippets are a way to show more information in a search result than normal, but it only applies to certain types of data. In particular, it is used for providing additional information on:
- Reviews
- Products
- Events
- People

- Restaurants

Here are some examples of rich snippets from Google:
Product rich snippets shows price, rating and review information:

> **adidas Rose 4.5 - Men's - Basketball - Shoes - White/White ...**
> www.eastbay.com/product/model.../sku.../adidas-rose-4.5.../black... ▼ Eastbay ▼
> ★★★★ Rating: 4.2 - 16 reviews - $139.99
> Get the **shoes** that help make D Rose one of the most explosive players in the game today. The **adidas Rose 4.5** will elevate your game while showing off flashy ...

Event rich snippets shows dates, location and name of event:

> **Little Shop Of Horrors Seattle Tickets - Excite**
> www.excite.com › ... › Little Shop Of Horrors Tickets ▼ Excite ▼
> Events@Excite is the perfect place to look for **Little Shop Of Horrors Seattle** Tickets. Not only do we have a huge tickets inventory, but also allow Absolute ...
>
> Tue, Jun 3   Little Shop Of Horrors Act ...   Act Theatre The Falls
> Wed, Jun 4   Little Shop Of Horrors Act ...   Act Theatre The Falls
> Thu, Jun 5   Little Shop Of Horrors Act ...   Act Theatre The Falls

Breadcrumbs rich snippets have links to the categories that the item falls in (Appliances > Small Appliances) instead of a URL:

> **Waffle Makers - Best Buy**
> www.bestbuy.com › Appliances › Small Appliances ▼ Best Buy ▼
> With a high-quality **waffle maker** from BestBuy.com, you can start y golden waffles. Get Free Shipping when you buy a **waffle maker** fro

Can you see how the additional information might make these search results stand out because they are different? Rich snippets are meant to provide details that are common for these search results. The search engines reward sites that provide such information by showing more information about them.

From an SEO perspective, attracting more eyes to these listings makes it more likely that they will get clicked on, and the higher the click-through rate (CTR – how often a person clicks on that search result), the more likely they are to move higher up in search results. So when one search result is getting a higher CTR than others, it indicates that it is more relevant to the keyword search than other results.

To implement rich snippets, you have to add code that labels relevant information to your pages.

There are different ways to mark the data as rich snippet relevant, but Schema.org is one we use because both Bing and Google have agreed to accept it as a standard, acceptable format (some formats are used by one, but not the other). Schema.org's site documents how objects should be labeled with code, along with examples.

Google also offers two valuable tools that help you implement rich snippets. The Google Structure Markup Data

Helper helps you create code for your pages, while the Google Structure Data Testing Tool tests that rich snippets are working correctly on your site.

Many sites still haven't implemented rich snippets, which gives you an opportunity to really stand out in search results if you do use them. Typically you have to pay to make your listing stand out in search results, so rich snippets are a great way to attract traffic without spending on ads.

6: Resources

Sitemaps

Google XML Sitemaps
(http://wordpress.org/plugins/google-sitemap-generator/) – A Wordpress plugin that creates a sitemap for you and automatically tells Google, Yahoo and Bing when you create a new page or change one.

XML-Sitemaps.com (http://www.xml-sitemaps.com/) – A free tool for creating a site map if you don't have software that makes one. Once the sitemap is created, you have to upload the file to your server and let the search engines know where it is located.

Webmaster Tools

Bing Webmaster Tools
(www.bing.com/toolbox/webmaster) – Allows website owners to tell Bing what's on their site (via sitemaps), see how Bing is crawling their site and learn what the search engine thinks the site is about.

Google Webmaster Tools
(http://google.com/webmaster/tools) – Allows website owners to tell Google what's on their site (via sitemaps), see how Google is crawling their site and learn what the search engine thinks the site is about.

Measure Page Load Speed

Google PageSpeed Insights (http://developers.google.com/speed/pagespeed/insights/) – Check how fast your website is loading and see recommendations for improvement by Google.

GT Metrix (http://gtmetrix.com/) – Similar to Google PageSpeed Insights, but GT Metrix provides many more recommendations and more analysis.

Improve Page Load Speed

Amazon Web Services - S3 (http://aws.amazon.com/s3/) – A service used by websites as a low cost way to store large files or ones that may get downloaded often by site visitors.

CloudFlare (http://cloudflare.com) – A content delivery network (CDN) that offers a free option.

Compressnow (http://compressnow.com/) – Upload images to compress them and make them a smaller size.

Online YUI Compressor (http://refresh-sf.com/yui/) – A tool that can minify JavaScript and CSS files you upload to your site.

JSCompress (http://jscompress.com/) – A JavaScript file minifier that combines .js (JavaScript) files.

WP Smush.it (http://wordpress.org/plugins/wp-smushit/) – A Wordpress plugin that compresses the size of images when they are uploaded to the website.

WP Supercache (http://wordpress.org/plugins/wp-supercache/) – A Wordpress plugin that caches content for faster page loading.

W3 Total Cache (http://wordpress.org/plugins/w3-total-cache/) – A Wordpress plugin that improves the site's performance with caching, minification and integrating with CDNs.

Rich Snippets

Google Structure Data Testing Tool
(http://www.google.com/webmasters/tools/richsnippets) – Tests that your rich snippets are correct for a web page.

Google Structure Markup Data Helper
(https://www.google.com/webmasters/markup-helper/) – Helps you do the coding for a web page to make rich snippets work.

Schema.org (http://schema.org) – Shows different types of rich snippets and how to code your pages to get the extra details to show in search results.

6: Actionable Checklist

- Did you create a sitemap for your website?
- Do you have Google Webmaster Tools set-up?
- Do you have Bing Webmaster Tools set-up?
- Is your sitemap location communicated in Google Webmaster Tools?
- Is your sitemap location communicated in Bing Webmaster Tools?
- How fast is your website loading?
- Are you minifying JavaScript and CSS files?
- Are you caching?
- Have you minimized any photos that are on your site?
- Do you have any information that you can use for rich snippets?

[7]

Keyword Research

Keyword research is essential in developing your digital marketing strategy. It will be used in determining what you'll try to rank for in search results, what content you'll put on your site, how you arrange your pages and the keywords you bid on if you choose to run paid ads.

While many keywords are obvious, many aren't (that may be really good ones).

Targeting the wrong keywords can cost you a lot of money. If a keyword is competitive (a lot of sites are trying to rank with the same words), you will have to spend more time and money trying to get ranked for it in SEO. In fact, you may never get ranked for the keyword and all of your investment could be for naught. It'll also cost you more each time someone clicks on it if you run paid ads since you need to outbid others to have your listing seen.

Here's an example using a florist. The obvious keywords – the ones that instantly come to mind – are "florist" and "flowers." When we look these words up in Google AdWords to get an idea of whether they might be good keywords, here's what we find:

While "florist" gets a lot of traffic, the level of competition is high:

Search terms	Avg. monthly searches	Competition	Suggested bid
florist	49,500	High	$5.60

The keyword "flowers" is worse; it's also highly competitive and costs almost 40% more:

Keyword (by relevance)	Avg. monthly searches	Competition	Suggested bid
flowers	673,000	High	$7.71

However, when we look down the list of suggestions, we find some other keywords that are good targets. They have decent search volume, little competition and their bid is about a third of the cost of "florist:"

Keyword (by relevance)	Avg. monthly searches	Competition	Suggested bid
flowers	673,000	High	$7.71
roses	165,000	Low	$1.50
flower	135,000	Medium	$5.07
flower delivery	135,000	High	$6.39
calla lily	60,500	Medium	$1.28
corsage	40,500	Low	$0.99
flowers.com	40,500	High	$4.87
wedding flowers	27,100	High	$1.39
purple flowers	27,100	Low	$1.95
bouquet	27,100	Low	$1.72

You're digging into the core structure of your offering to focus on what sets you apart from all the other "florists" out there.

Even if you're not going to be running Google ads, this is important data because it's typically indicative of not only the level of competition for paid search, but also SEO. In other words, if a lot of people are clamoring to pay to get visitors who search for that keyword, then you had better believe they are also competing to get free traffic for it. Furthermore, the number of monthly searches gives you an idea of the amount of possible business you could drum up by targeting a particular keyword.

Google's Keyword Planner Tool is one of many routes you can take for researching keywords. Here we're going to show you different tactics for determining which keywords you'll use in your digital marketing strategy. As you're going through the exercises we show you, make sure that you're keeping a record of these keywords in a file (i.e. Word, Excel, notepad, etc.).

Your Data

The first place to look for keyword ideas is in your data to see what has attracted people to your site in the past and what things your site visitors are most interested in. Google Analytics, Google Webmaster Tools, and Bing Webmaster Tools make this easy.

Google Analytics

Keywords - Organic Report – This report shows queries that are ranking for your site in Google and how long visitors are staying (who were referred by that keyword).

(1) On the left navigation menu, go to *Acquisition > Keywords > Organic:*

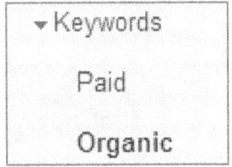

(2) Click on the column headers to sort:

Keyword	Acquisition			Behavior		
	Sessions ↓	% New Sessions	New Users	Bounce Rate	Pages / Session	Avg. Session Duration
	5,776 % of Total 18.43% (31,348)	60.34% Site Avg 61.09% (-1.24%)	3,485 % of Total 18.20% (19,151)	23.18% Site Avg 28.56% (-12.66%)	4.40 Site Avg 3.41 (29.21%)	00:03:51 Site Avg 00:02:44 (40.79%)
1.	4,737 (82.01%)	60.46%	2,864 (82.18%)	23.69%	4.38	00:03:48
2.	217 (3.76%)	49.77%	108 (3.10%)	17.51%	4.50	00:03:57
3.	155 (2.68%)	63.87%	99 (2.84%)	12.90%	5.06	00:04:26
4.	84 (1.45%)	78.57%	66 (1.89%)	5.95%	4.45	00:03:49

In this report, note that:
- Keywords that are leading to the highest "Pages/Session" and "Avg. Session Duration" indicates content that people are interested in.
- Keywords with the lowest bounce rates indicate that people found what they were looking for when they clicked on your search result (bounce rate is how often someone visited a page and immediately left the page).

Search Engine Optimization - Queries Report – This report shows queries that are ranking for your site in Google, and how often people are clicking on your search result.

(1) On the menu on the left, go to *Acquisition > Search Engine Optimization > Queries*:

(2) Click on the column headers to sort the results:

Query	Impressions	↓ Clicks	Average Position	CTR
	11,098 % of Total: 73.89% (15,100)	2,283 % of Total: 76.10% (3,000)	7.1 Site Avg: 19 (-64.00%)	20.57% Site Avg: 20.00% (2.09%)
1.	2,500 (22.53%)	700 (30.66%)	1.1	28.00%
2.	2,000 (18.02%)	320 (14.02%)	3.0	16.00%
3.	900 (8.11%)	170 (7.45%)	2.5	18.89%
4.	900 (8.11%)	400 (17.52%)	1.0	44.44%
5.	400 (3.60%)	110 (4.82%)	1.0	27.50%
6.	200 (1.80%)	50 (2.19%)	1.3	25.00%

In this report, note that:
- Keywords that are getting high click-through rates or a high volume of clicks indicate people are interested in this content on your site.
- Where you show in search – if you're ranking high and getting clicks, you will want to make sure that you maintain this position, and if you're ranking low for something with a high amount of "Impressions," you may want to target this keyword because it could bring traffic if you move up.

Google Webmaster Tools
Links to Your Site Report – This report shows what content people are linking to and what words they are using to link to you. These linked words, often referred to as **anchor text**, can provide you clues as to keywords you might want to target.

In addition, links to your site show that people find this content valuable, therefore help your search rankings. Include more content like this to attract more links.

(1) On the menu on the left, go to *Search Traffic > Links to Your Site*:

(2) Click on any of the More links for additional results:

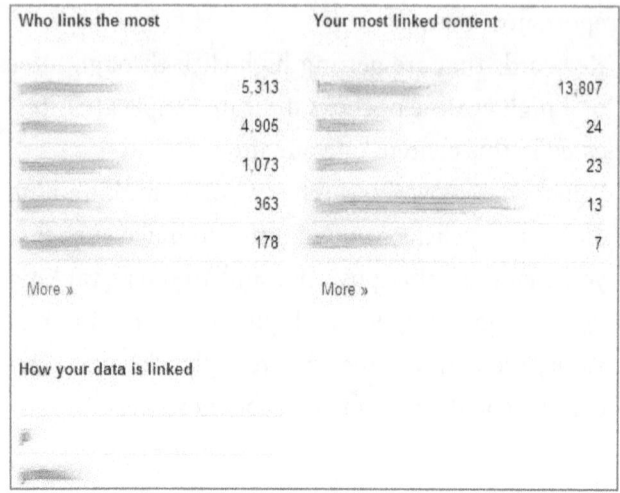

In this report, note that:
- Anchor text in the "How your data is linked" can give you hints to keywords that people might be interested in.
- The URLs that show in "Your most linked content" – if you add more content like this, you can attract more links.

Bing Webmaster Tools
Search Keywords Report – This report shows keywords that are ranking for your site in Bing and Yahoo, and how often people are clicking on your search result.

(1) On the menu on the left, go to *Reports & Data > Search Keywords:*

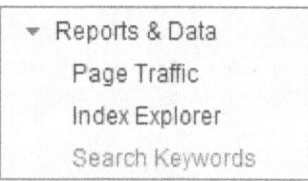

Make Money on the Internet | 153

(2) Click on the column headers to sort the results:

KEYWORDS	CLICKS FROM SEARCH	APPEARED IN SEARCH	CLICK-THROUGH RATE	AVG SEARCH CLICK POSITION	AVG SEARCH APPEARANCE POSITION	SERVED PAGES
▓▓▓▓▓	0	10	0%		5.5	(View)
▓▓▓▓▓	0	7	0%		5.5	(View)
▓▓▓▓▓	0	6	0%		16.5	(View)
▓▓▓▓▓	0	4	0%		3.5	(View)
▓▓▓▓▓	0	4	0%		2.0	(View)
▓▓▓▓▓	0	4	0%		19.0	(View)

In this report, note:

- Keywords that are getting high click-through rates or a high volume of clicks indicate people are interested in this content on your site.
- Where you show in search – If you're ranking high and getting clicks, you want to make sure that you maintain this position, and if you're ranking low for something with a high amount of "Appeared in Search," you may want to target this keyword because it could bring traffic if you move up.

Page Traffic Report – This report shows pages that are receiving traffic from searches on Bing and Yahoo.

(1) On the menu on the left, go to *Reports & Data > Page Traffic*:

(2) Click on the column headers to sort the results:

PAGE	CLICKS FROM SEARCH	APPEARED IN SEARCH	CLICK THROUGH RATE	AVG SEARCH CLICK POSITION	AVG SEARCH APPEARANCE POSITION	SEARCH KEYWORDS
	0	98	0 %		24.8	(View)
	0	53	0 %		21.9	(View)
	2	51	3.02 %	3.0	5.3	(View)
	0	29	0 %		25.0	(View)
	0	14	0 %		25.2	(View)
	0	12	0 %		21.5	(View)
	0	10	0 %		15.5	(View)

In this report:
- Pages that are getting high click-through rates or a high volume of clicks indicate people are interested in this content on your site.

Competitive Research

It's important to keep tabs on your competitors so you can take what's working for them and use it to your advantage in your business.

In terms of SEO, when you start competing for keywords that your competitors are ranking well for, you can start to steal of some of their prospective business and increase your traffic.

Alexa is a website that provides information on websites to you for free. One particularly useful piece of SEO information it provides is the **keywords that bring the site the most traffic.**

Top Keywords from Search Engines	
Which search keywords send traffic to this site?	
Keyword	Percent of Search Traffic
1. espn	12.73%
2. nba	1.19%
3. nfl	0.90%
4. monday night football	0.59%
5. espn nba	0.46%

In this example for espn.com, you can see the top keywords and how much of the search traffic each particular one delivers.

The advantage to having this type of knowledge should be obvious to you by this point, and can be valuable when you're mapping out your SEO strategy.

Follow.net is a free tool that works directly in your browser. You simply download the software, sign-up for a free account and then visit competitor websites. An icon will now appear on your browser bar.

(1) Whenever you visit a competitor, click on the Follow.net icon at the top of your browser to see valuable keyword information.

(2) In the SEO section of the pop-up that appears, you'll see what the top keywords are for the site based on different software. The results will differ since each has its own way of determining top keywords, which makes Follow.net useful since it shows results from different sources, giving your more knowledge and insight.

Keyword	Google Rank	Yahoo / Bing Rank
3	4	100
4	6	100
5	7	100
6	8	100

In the search engine marketing (SEM) section, you can see what keywords they're running ads for, which shows that they feel confident that these are good words for bringing in traffic:

Keyword	Days	Volume	Avg CPC
4	55	1,900	$ 1.93
5	4	880	$ 0.89
6	1	590	$ 0.35
7	1	260	$ 0.54
8	1	260	$ 0.88
9	3	170	$ 0.68
10	1	46	$ 1.14

While Follow.net shows a fair amount of data for free (70%), you'll have to pay to see all of it. One example is, as you look through the results with a free account, you'll notice that the results don't start with the #1 keyword, but usually #3 or #4. So you'll have to pay if you want to see the top results. But even going with the free account initially will prove extremely useful.

Keyword Tools

Suggestion Tools

There are lots of keyword tools that you can use to get suggestions if you need a kick start. Most keyword suggestion tools are paid (with some offering a free trial), but one you can use for free is **Ubersuggest** (which gets its money through ads). Similar to other tools, you just type in a keyword into a search box, and then the tool spits out suggestions for alternatives.

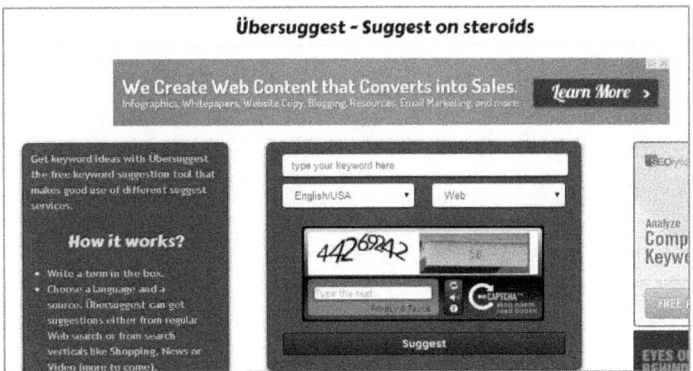

To run an Ubersuggest search, simply:

(1) Enter your keyword, the reCaptcha code (to prove you're a human), and then click the *Suggest* button.

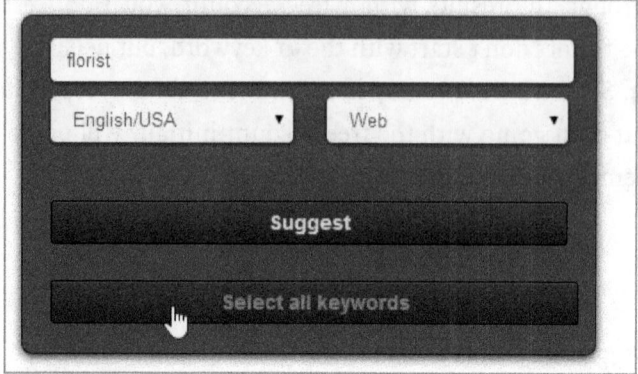

(2) After the results appear, you can select all of them by clicking *Select all keywords* or click the "+" icon to the left of the suggested keyword to indicate you're interested in this keyword:

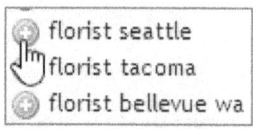

(3) On the right side, click the Get button to make a pop-up appear with all of the words you were interested in.

(4) In the pop-up window, highlight all of the keywords and then copy and paste them into a Word document to save them.

```
Copy & Paste

florist
florist seattle
florist tacoma
florist bellevue wa
florist issaquah
florist near me
florist puyallup wa
florist salem oregon
florist olympia wa
florist redmond wa
florist scranton pa
florist stroudsburg pa
florist wilkes barre pa
florist east stroudsburg pa
florist dallas pa
florist in hazleton pa
```

Google Keyword Planner

As we saw earlier, the **Google Keyword Planner Tool** can be extremely helpful in finding keywords. The tool is a part of *Google's AdWords* platform, which is where ads can be purchased for the search engine. You don't need to pay to use the tool, it's free, but you do have to sign-up for an account.

(1) Once you sign-up for an account, on the top menu go to *Tools > Keyword Planner*.

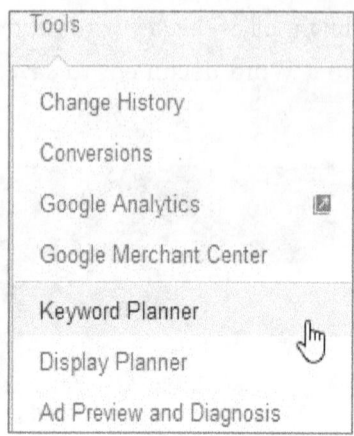

(2) Once in the Keyword Planner, click on the first option for Search for new keyword and ad group ideas.

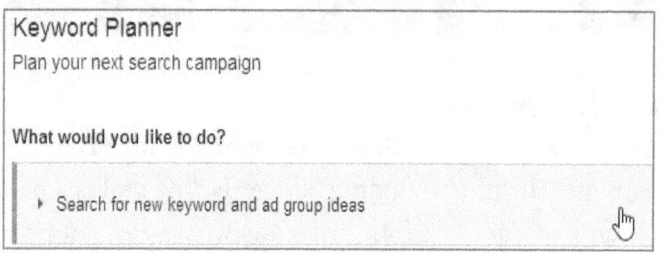

(3) In the *Your product or service* field, paste or type the keywords you found earlier.

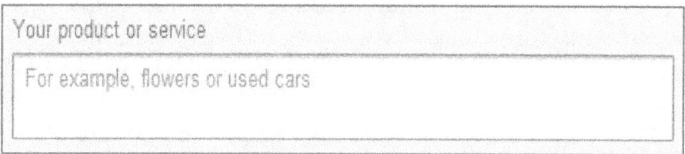

(4) (Optional) If your customers are in a certain geographical location, you will want to change the target from the

default of "United States," otherwise you're going to see the search volumes of people across the country, as opposed to just your local area (i.e. your target market).

a. Click the box that says *United States*.

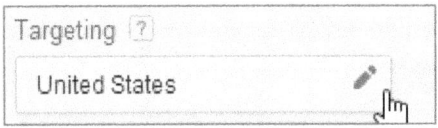

b. Click the *Remove* link to the right of United States:

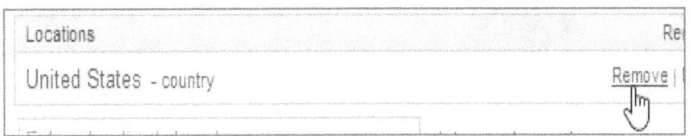

c. In the location box, enter the area (city, county, state or country) you want to target (you can do as many as you want).

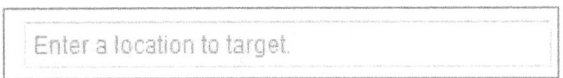

d. If you're planning on adding multiple places that are next to each other, you can add one and then click *Nearby* to quickly add other locations.

For example, once we enter Seattle, we can click *Nearby*:

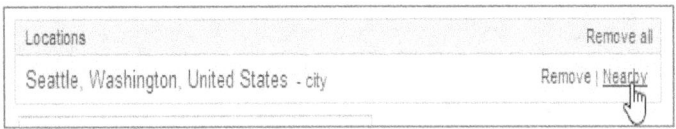

A pop-up is then shown with nearby locations, and the *Add* button can be clicked for many locations at once (click *Done* when all nearby locations are selected).

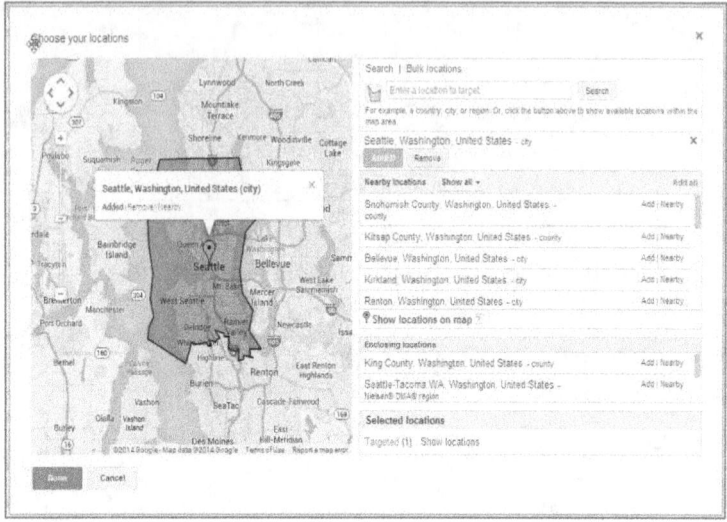

(5) Click *Get ideas* to see Google's suggestions.

(6) Once the results display, click on the *Keyword ideas* tab:

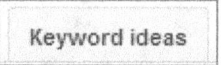

(7) From here, you'll see the keyword suggestions which you can sort by clicking a column, or you can click *Download* to sort them in Excel.

Primary targets are keywords that have low or medium competition and good search volume (relative to the other keywords in the list).

To sort the list by competition level, in the *Keyword (by relevance)* section, click on the column for *Competition* so that the arrow is pointing up. After it sorts, look through the list to see which of the low and medium competition level keywords are relevant to you, and which ones have decent traffic.

You may also want to look for keywords that you saw in Google that you're placing in the top 100-150 for, and for which you receive a worthwhile amount of traffic. These would be keywords that, with work, you might be able to rank higher for (and receive traffic from).

7: Resources

Keyword Research

Alexa (http://alexa.com) – View traffic information for your competitors, including what keywords are bringing them the most search traffic.

Bing Keyword Tool (http://www.bing.com/toolbox/keywords) – Use Bing's advertising platform to get keyword ideas (and see search volumes). You don't need to run a paid campaign to use the tool. Tip: When signing up for an account, do a search for Bing ad coupons to see if you can get free ad credits (coupons usually must be applied within a certain amount of days of opening an account).

Follow.net (http://follow.net) – See what keywords competitors are talking about in search engine optimization (SEO) and search engine marketing (SEM).

Google Keyword Planner Tool (http://google.com/AdWords) – Part of the Google AdWords platform which you can use for free, you can get suggestions from Google on keywords and see estimates for monthly search traffic. Tip: When signing up for an account, do a search for AdWords coupons to see if you can get free ad credits (coupons usually must be applied within a certain amount of days of opening an account).

Keyword Eye (http://www.keywordeye.com/) – They offer a free plan where you can run 10 keyword searches per day to get ideas on what you should be targeting with your SEO.

Ubersuggest (http://ubersuggest.org) – A free tool that allows you to receive keyword suggestions.

Wordstream (http://www.wordstream.com/keywords) – Offers a limited number of free searches you can do for keywords.

7: Actionable Checklist

- What keywords are bringing you the most search traffic?
- Which keywords lead to the most conversions on your site?
- Which keywords are you ranked high for?
- What keywords could you add that you're not already using?
- Are there keywords bringing you traffic, but you're ranked low for (and could possibly move up)?
- What keywords are bringing your competitors the most traffic?
- What keywords are your competitors advertising for?

[8]
On Page SEO

When Google or Bing crawl your site, they are looking at your web pages and trying to understand what they are about – they're peeking behind the curtain to the structure of your site. The search engines then determine what keywords the pages might relate to. Similar to publishing a sitemap, there are things you can do with your site to help search engines understand what your pages are about – this is **On Page SEO**.

Tag, I'm It

While the code for web pages is all going to be different, there are some common tags that are used. Tags are pieces of code that communicate information that is relevant to the page, but don't necessarily appear on the page.

Why are they important then?

Tags communicate to search engines what the page is about.

Title Tag
The **title tag** is the most important one for SEO purposes. It shows on the top of the browser tab and is used to provide an overview of the page. You should carefully think about the title because search engines key off of it to determine the subject of the page.

The title tag in the code appears in the <head> section of the code, near the top:

> <title>Think Strategy - Web Development and Design, SEO, SEM, Sales Funnels</title>

The title tag in search results:

Think Strategy - Web Development and Design, SEO, SEM ...
thinkstrategy.com
We drive online sales and leads for our clients by offering SEO, SEM, web development and sales funnel management. Contact us for a free consultation.

Tips for your title tag:
- Google displays about 50-60 characters (depending on the width of the letters – an "o" will take up more space than an "I"), so make sure that any text you want to show in the search results is less than 50-55 characters long.
- While you don't want your title to be too long, you do want to use as much of the space that the search engines give you so you can provide adequate details about your page.
- It should include the keyword(s) you're targeting for the page, preferably as close to the start of the title as possible.
- It should be enticing to click on for people seeing it in search results to improve your listing's click-through rate.

Meta Description Tag

The **meta description tag** doesn't show on a web page. It used to be for search engines to get a long description about a page, but now it's used mainly for displaying in search results under the title and URL.

> **Think Strategy** - Web Development and Design, SEO, SEM ...
> thinkstrategy.com/
> We drive online sales and leads for our clients by offering SEO, SEM, web development and sales funnel management. Contact us for a free consultation.

It shows in the <head> section of the code near the top, under the <title> tag, and will look something like this:

```
<meta name="description" content="We drive online sales and leads for our clients by offering SEO, SEM, web development and sales funnel management. Contact us for a free consultation."/>
```

Tips for the meta description tag:
- Google displays about 150-160 characters (depending on the width of the letters), so make sure that any text you want to show in the search results is less than 150-155 characters long.
- While you don't want your meta description to be too long, you want to use as much of the space that the search engines give you so you can provide adequate details about your page.
- It should include the keyword(s) you're targeting for the page.
- It should be enticing to click on for people seeing it in search results to improve your listing's click-through rate.

Don't Do This
Search engine algorithms used to rely heavily on the count of keyword mentions... that was long ago. What happened was, people who were trying to "game" the system added a bunch of keywords to not only the web page, but also to the tags.

Google doesn't like it when people try to game the system.

It won't help you if you try to mention the same keyword repeatedly through the title and description. In fact, that's the type of thing that Google might penalize you for. So not only does it have a negative effect on users, but it looks funny to read "Sunglasses, Cheap Sunglasses, Ray Ban Sunglasses, Women's Sunglasses, and Men's Sunglasses" as the title for a web page. If you were normally writing this, you'd write it as "Cheap, Ray Ban, Women's, and Men's Sunglasses" instead.

In its algorithm behind the scenes, Google tries to look for text like this to penalize (lower them in search rankings) because it's not written well (which leads to a poorer user experience) and the site is likely trying to keyword stuff (jamming in keywords for the sole purpose of trying to move up in rankings = a no-no).

Once you're on Google's bad side, it's not always easy to recover, so try and keep your powder dry.

Are You Heading Google's Way?
Headlines are another thing that Google and Bing use to understand what your web page is about. We mentioned these a while ago, but let's look at them in a little more detail now. Again, if you're managing your own website, this will be very valuable information so make sure you pay attention. If you have someone else helping to manage your

site, it's important that you know about these things so that you can communicate exactly what you want them to do for your site.

To properly cite a header, use the <H1> to <H6> tags in the <body> section of the code,

The most important headline, the main one, is <H1>, with each subsequent number indicating a less important headline. From a search engine perspective, they only care about <H1> and <H2>.

Use these to tags provide an outline for your users and the search engines. The main headline (H1) summarizes the content for the page, while the subheadlines (H2) break down the content into smaller, logical topics.

Tips for the H1 and H2 tags:

- The H1 should include the keyword(s) you're targeting for the page.
- The H2 can include the keyword you're targeting, but it doesn't have to - you may also consider using something which is a variation of the keyword in the H2 (for example, if your keyword is "microwave" and you have it in your H1, maybe your H2 mentions "small appliance" instead).

Reading Photos

While a picture may not say a thousand words to Google yet since the search engine can't "see" it, a picture still has its say.

The **alt attribute** is an optional setting for images that many websites neglect to use. Or if it is used, too often the alt attribute is not specified or is not well thought out. That's too bad.

Search engines use the alt tag to understand what the image is about. Not only does this help the picture get found by people doing images searches, but it's another important clue as to what the page is about.

Here's an example of from a page on National Geographic's site on birds. When we look at the code, we can see that all of the images use the alt attribute to specify the bird's name. The fact that all of the pictures on the page are about birds and each are labeled with a bird's name (using the alt attribute) is a strong indicator to search engines that the page is about the feathered creatures even without reading any text displayed on the page.

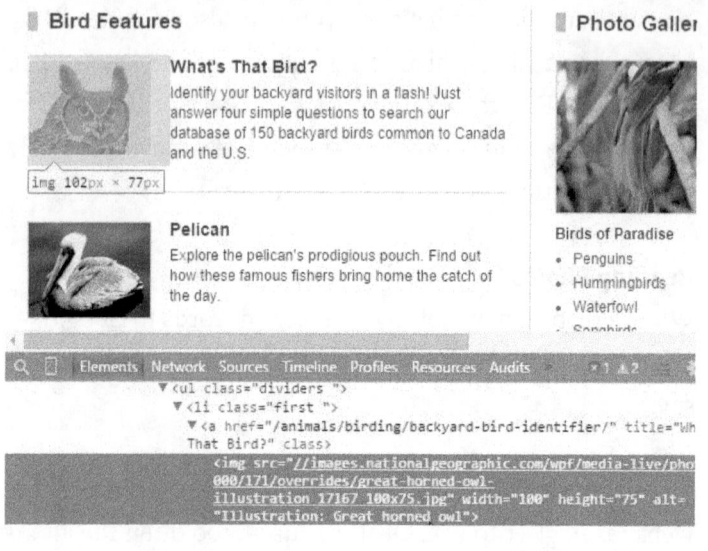

Tips for the alt attribute:

- Make sure that you specify some text for each image.
- If possible and if it makes sense, use the keyword(s) you're targeting in the text for the alt attribute.

8: Resources

SEO On Page Analysis Tools

Image SEO Tool (http://www.feedthebot.com/tools/alt/) – Checks images on a web page to see if they are tagged for SEO (i.e. use alt tag).

Meta Length (http://www.metalength.com/) – Counts the characters you enter for your meta tags so you can make sure they are as descriptive as possible without being too long.

Microsoft Free SEO Tool (http://www.microsoft.com/web/seo) – A free tool from Microsoft that gives SEO suggestions.

SEOmofo (http://www.seomofo.com/snippet-optimizer.html) – A cool tool that will show you what your web page will look like in Google in search results as you enter your meta tags.

Wordpress SEO (https://wordpress.org/plugins/wordpress-seo/) – The most comprehensive SEO plugin for Wordpress. It checks posts for search engine ranking factors for a specified keyword, and creates and manages sitemaps.

8: Actionable Checklist

- Have you reviewed all of your title tags and included your keyword(s)?
- Is your title attractive, encouraging people to click on it in search results?
- Is your title a good length?
- Is your meta description attractive, encouraging people to click on in search results?
- Is your meta description a good length?
- Are you using H1 and H2 tags in your content to provide an outline for search engines?
- Have you specified the alt attribute for all images?

[9]

Getting Found in Local Search

One specific area of SEO that is often overlooked is local search. So often business owners focus on the big Internet picture so much that they fail to focus on boosting their local Internet presence.

What search engines realized is that a lot of the time when someone searches for businesses, they're interested in finding someone local. For example, if you start a search for a veterinarian, you're probably looking for one who is local, even if you didn't specify a location in your search (i.e. "*Seattle* veterinarian").

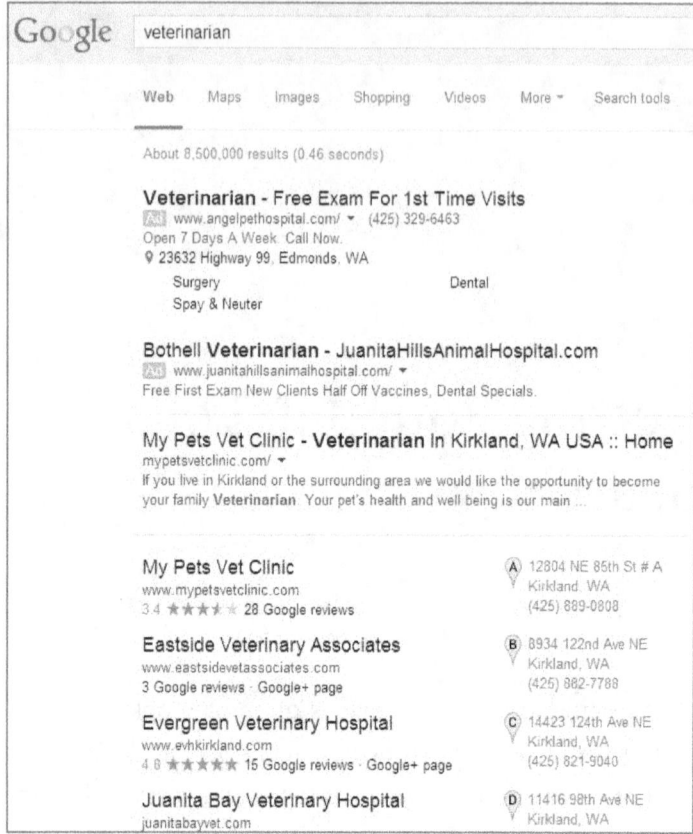

Therefore, search engines started to include local businesses in the search, whether an area was specified or not.

What may be even more compelling is that studies have shown how likely people are to buy after conducting a local search. According to a study by Ipsos MediaCT, 34% of consumers who searched for local information on their computer or tablet made their way to a store, and of those who used a smartphone, the number is an astounding 50%[3]. Another study by comScore, Neustar Localeze and 15 Miles points to an even higher number, with 78% of local searches on mobile devices resulting in purchases[4].

In this section, we'll give you tips on how to boost your rank in local searches.

Making Your Site More Local

We've already talked earlier about the importance of including your address and phone number on your site to establish trust. Doing this also helps with local search. If a search engine crawls your site and doesn't find an address, how do you expect to rank higher in local searches?

Make sure that your address appears on your site, but also that it's in text form. Sometimes, the address may appear as an image. When it's an image, search engines can't read it (we just discussed this in the last step, remember?).

Another place to include your address is in the footer of the page. This will give search engines additional exposure to your address.

---

[3] Google/Ipsos MediaCT/Purchased, Research: Understanding Consumers' Local Search Behavior, May 2014

[4] comScore, Neustar Localeze, 15 Miles. 9 April 2014. *Local Search Study*. Retrieved 3 June 2014, from http://www.localsearchstudy.com/local_search_study_2013.pdf.

Consider focusing some pages on local content. For example, if you support any local non-profits, you may want to include a blog post on that. Or maybe there are some local events that you want to promote – more blog fodder that could help communicate to search engines where you are.

Get Listed

For local search, a lot of the work that needs to be done takes place outside of your website.

The first thing you should do is to make sure that you're listed in major local directories - most of which are free to be in (although some are paid). The most popular ones are Yelp, Foursquare, Google Places, and Citysearch. And while it's not a directory, Facebook is a place that search engines rely on for addresses, so make sure you have a page with those details.

These sites are important for local search because they have developed a solid reputation from Google and Bing as being good directories. You may find, after a quick check, that they list your site already. If that's the case, make sure you claim your listing. If you don't find your site on them, make it a priority to log in and create a listing. The overall process for registering your business is similar for all of these sites.

1. Fill out a simple form on the site with details about your business, including:

a. Name
   b. Contact information
   c. Business category
   d. Hours of Operation
   e. Pictures of your business
2. After you submit the form, the directory will try to verify your business by sending a postcard with a code on it.
3. When you receive the postcard, go online and enter the verification code to make your listing live.

The main thing to remember when creating these listings is that **you must be consistent**. The name, address and phone (NAP) must match between your website and all of these listings in order for you to reap all the benefits.

For example, if you create these two listings...

Linda's Awesome Accountants
202 Westminster Street West
Dublin, OH 77103
(800) 355-7252

Linda's Awesome Accountants, LLC
202 Westminster St W
Dublin, OH 77103
602-452-0023

...you're not going to rate as high in local search as you would if everything was consistent. In essence, you've created what might be construed by search engines as two different locations/businesses. Keep everything the same across the Internet so that each listing adds to your local search rank.

Also, try to make your listing as complete as possible. Add your hours of operation and pictures even though it's optional. Choose as many business categories as applicable for you – most of the listing sites allow at least 3-5 categories per business. Each additional bit of information is something picked up by search engines and increase the likelihood you'll be found by a prospective customer.

What Others Think

On your website you use testimonials to build trust with visitors. On these local listing sites, **reviews** act as the currency. You want to build positive reviews because (a) it helps you form your reputation with prospective customers, and (b) it shows that you have customers. It's nice if 100% of your reviews are positive, but it may not go that far if you only have a grand total of two reviews.

Increasing the Number Of Reviews

As you could probably guess, people are generally not inspired to leave a review unless they are upset about something.

You need to actively look for ways to encourage people to write reviews. Don't be hesitant to come right out and ask for a review. Let them know that you're on Yelp (and the other sites) to remind them that others are anxiously waiting to hear their opinion on your business.

Here are a few ideas to get you started:

1. If you can, place signage near the exit (or cash register) so people are reminded to submit a review as they leave your location

2. Print a reminder to leave a review on your receipts.
3. Have printed cards displayed in your office.

4. Have a link on your website to the review page for your listing.
5. Encourage check-ins with signage.

6. Put a link in your newsletters.
7. Create and host a Yelp event (http://www.yelp.com/events).

Don't Do This

You can encourage people to do reviews, but don't bribe them. Bribing is against the terms and conditions on listing sites, not to mention that it's against the whole spirit of trying to create an environment where people air their honest opinions. This includes offering discounts for reviews.

Also, ask for reviews in general, not specifically for positive ones. Again, try to stay on the good side of the directories that want to maintain their integrity.

Responding To Negative Feedback

The more reviews you get, the higher the chance that you're going to receive negative feedback. It's going to happen.

While you may be tempted to disregard or ignore a negative review, that's the worst thing you can do. First, it's an opportunity to learn about things you can do to improve your business. Second, when comments aren't responded to, readers may come to accept it as the truth and think you don't care that someone has a negative opinion about your business.

The first thing is you should try to develop a process where you regularly check in on places where people can write reviews about you. Depending on the volume you typically receive, set your schedule accordingly. If people leave you new reviews daily or weekly, check at least weekly. If they leave reviews less frequently, then take a quick peek monthly.

If you find a negative comment, make sure you read it. The most natural reaction is to get angry, embarrassed or feel rejected. After reading it, resist replying to the comment immediately. This gives you a chance to let the emotions subside and gives you a chance to respond in a level-headed way.

If the complaint(s) sounds legitimate, remember that just like no person is perfect, no business is perfect. Try not to get too worked up about it. Learn from it and adapt to get better. Respond back apologizing for the bad experience, offer to fix it and perhaps let them know why it happened.

There are definitely going to be people who are simply unreasonable with their expectations as customers. Some like to say that 20% of people will like you no matter what, while another 20% will dislike you no matter what. If the complaint is unreasonable, go the extra step to tell them that you're sorry that they had poor experience and that you'd like to earn their business back.

You want to avoid getting defensive to the point that you look hostile (which doesn't lend itself well to a prospective customer doing business with you). You will look ornery if you berate the commenter (even if it's unreasonable feedback) or if you don't prove that you're willing to be more accommodating (by explaining why the bad experience happened or what changes you've made to prevent it happening in the future). People understand that you're human and that you may make mistakes, but they won't want to deal with you if you seem unfriendly, angry and spiteful.

9: Resources

Directories

Make sure you're listed in these directories to boost your results in local search. If you have multiple locations, be sure to list each individually. Just make sure you don't create duplicate listings for a location in a directory or you'll hurt your search rankings.

Bing Places (https://www.bingplaces.com/)

DexKnows (http://dexknows.com)

Facebook (http://facebook.com) (include your address and number on your Facebook page profile)

Foursquare (http://foursquare.com)

Google Local (http://www.google.com/local/add/businessCenter)

HotFrog (http://hotfrog.com)

Localeze (http://neustarlocaleze.biz)

Manta (http://manta.com)

SuperPages (http://superpages.com)

Yelp (http://yelp.com)

YP (http://yp.com)

Listing Tools

If you have a lot of locations, you might find it worthwhile to use software to make sure you're listed everywhere, and with the same details.

Moz Local (https://moz.com/local)

Single Platform (http://www.singleplatform.com/)

Yext (http://www.yext.com/)

9: Actionable Checklist

- Is your contact information on your site in text so it's readable by search engines?
- Are you listed in the directories found in the Resources section?
- Have you claimed your business on sites where it's already listed?
- Is your name, address and phone exactly the same on each of the listings?
- Are you consistently encouraging people to write reviews?
- Are you monitoring and responding to your reviews regularly?

Part Three

Time to Get Social

[10]

Social Media Rules of Engagement

Social media can be an effective source for web sales and leads. Hundreds of millions of people use social media daily and it can be a great way to soft sell potential customers. When people are sold too aggressively they may shut down and avoid listening to any messages from businesses.

Social media tends to be more casual than other methods of communication, which leads to conversations, engagement and relationship building if done right.

Social media sets an environment where businesses can be friends with customers and prospects by providing entertainment and valuable content, as opposed to someone constantly trying to take your money. In exchange, consumers let down their guard more – listening to what businesses say (and have to offer).

By developing relationships, businesses start to occupy mind share. That is, people start to associate certain products and services to certain companies. Wouldn't it be nice if every time a potential customer thought about a product or service you offer, they automatically thought of your business first?

While each social media site is a little bit unique, there are some basic principles and concepts that can be applied to all of them.

But here is, perhaps, one of the most important things to remember about social media for your business**: it doesn't cost you anything to have a strong social media presence**. Nothing.

Sure, you can pay to have professional profile images created and you can pay to run ads on social media, but those things are not necessary to get started. You can literally set your business up at no cost, other than your time. You will invest some time each day or week maintaining engagement and building followers, but again, at no out-of-pocket expense. So social media should be a strong part of any business' advertising and marketing strategy from day one (or maybe even before then).

GETTING TO KNOW YOU

Similar to your website, you only have a few seconds to make an impression on a visitor with social media, so make it count. Make sure that your profile looks professional and tells them what you do immediately. In other words, **give them a reason to "Like" you [literally].**

While each social media site has a different layout, they all have a lot in common.

Let's first take a look at **Facebook**. Here, when someone types in or clicks on your name or the name of your business, the first things they see at your page are your cover and profile images. It's really not much different than with your personal pages, where you have a profile image and a cover image. Now you're just adjusting your perspective towards your business.

Typically, the **profile image** is your company logo or an image that is representative of your business. The **cover im-**

age, on the other hand, allows you to be creative while telling your story. It's a large, prominent piece of real estate, so put some thought into making it an attractive, eye-catching image. You can add text to it, but don't add too much. Being too wordy can discourage people from reading the text and minimize the impact of the cover image. Remember, this is not your webpage.

Here are some creative ways to tell your story with your cover image:

Display some of the products you currently have available (i.e. seasonal specials or product lines):

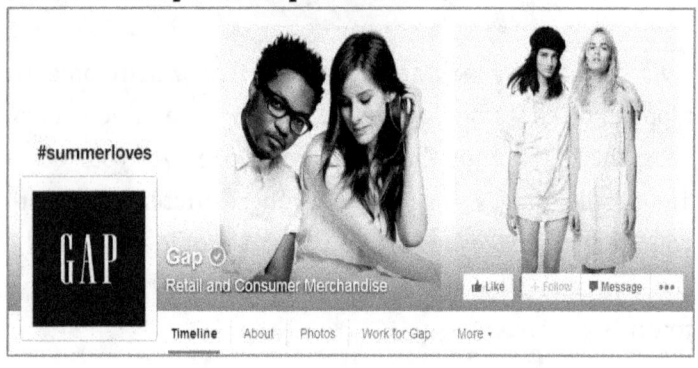

A tagline and an image showing what you do, or who you are:

198 | *Make Money on the Internet*

Promote an event:

In your actual profile, make sure that you also complete as many of the fields as possible. These details help people find you while doing searches and tell why visitors should become a fan – it's part of your story.

As we mentioned earlier, specific to Facebook, the address and phone help by not only informing visitors of your contact information, but it also helps in local search.

There are almost an unlimited number of things you can do to engage your audience. Just makes sure that your choices reinforce what your business does.

Build On What You Have

After you complete your profile (remember, now we're talking about social media sites as a whole), it's time to build up your fan base and followers to maximize your reach. This represents how many people will receive your content. Over time, your following will grow organically if you regularly post quality content. However, you most likely want to actively work to increase the number, especially when you are first establishing your presence.

The first source of fans should be your current, known supporters. Empty out your email address books and invite all of your contacts that may be interested in following you. Let people who are on your email and newsletter lists know about your social media sites and encourage them to become your fans. They've already shown an interest in following what you have to say. Make it as easy for them as possible to become your online friend by including links to your social media profiles in highly visible places (on your website, in your email signature, in electronic newsletters or white papers) and showing the complete URL in places where links don't make sense (i.e. in a paper newsletter or on signage).

Here are a few other ideas to attract more online supporters:

- Add the links to your email signature.
- Put up signage in your business with the URL to your social profiles.

- Place your URL on print and/or emailed receipts.
- Include the URL on your business cards.
- "Tag" photos you post with people's names so it shows in their feeds.

On your website, build in the ability to share, where it makes sense (i.e. content) and have links to your social media profiles so it is easy for someone to become a follower. Links to social profiles are often placed near the top of the page or the bottom as links using the icon of the particular site.

For example, on Jamba Juice, they place links to their social media profiles at the top:

And in their footer:

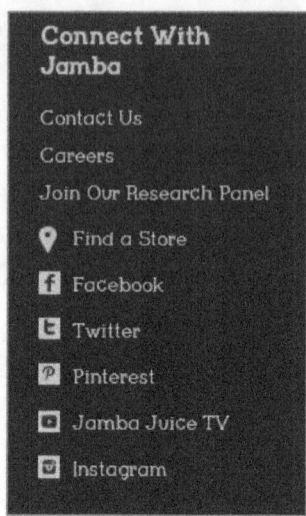

To encourage sharing, they place the appropriate links near the top of the content they want shared (generally a blog, tips, photos):

Similarly, on Nautica's site, they include profile links in the footer:

And they encourage people to share right on the page of specific products:

The rise of social media (and sharing) has ushered in plenty of free tools to make it easy to add social sharing functionality to your site. If you're using Wordpress, there are plugins that you can use so you don't need to know any code. Other tools typically require you to copy and paste a small snippet of code to make sharing buttons work.

When And What To Post

The type of content to share on social media will vary depending on the site, but many of the principles on what to post remain the same no matter what. Share things that will be of interest to your customer persona and mix it up between content that they'd find entertaining or informative, and any announcements or plugs for your product/service. Whenever possible, post photos because they catch people's attention and they lead to higher engagement rates (and will get shared by others more often).

The automobile service company, Midas, uses social media to entertain people with light-hearted humor while reminding you about what they do. Can you see how someone who is into cars may like them?

Make Money on the Internet | 205

Midas
May 16

Don't be that guy.

Midas
May 29

"For the last time, I am NOT asking for directions."

Like Comment Share   6 Shares

Time It Just Right

Since people can get inundated with posts on social media, it's easy for them to miss what you have to say. To improve the chances of your posts getting seen, try to send things during the times when your fans and followers are most likely to see it.

Fannit, an Internet marketing firm, conducted research to determine when were the best times for postings[5]. Here are their findings:

Facebook:
Best times – Weekdays from 6-8 AM and 2-5 PM
Worst times – 10 PM-4 AM

Twitter:
Best times – 1-3 PM, especially on weekends
Worst times – 8 PM-8 AM

Google+:
Best times – 9-11 AM
Worst times – 6 PM-7 AM

LinkedIn:
Best times – 7-8:30 AM, 5-6 PM

---

[5] Campbell, Isaac. 9 September 2013. *Best Times to Post on Social Media – Free Tips in New Infographic*. Retrieved 11 June 2014, from http://fannit.com/social-media-infographic-when-are-the-best-times-to-post/.

Worst times – Monday and Friday, and 9 AM-5 PM

Pinterest:
Best times – Saturday morning, 2-4 PM and 8-11 PM
Worst times – 5-7 PM and 1-7 AM

It's not always easy to post at the right time, fortunately there's software like Hootsuite to help make it easier. **Hootsuite** is a free tool (depending on how many social media accounts you post to) that you can use for scheduling your posts in advance, during these premium times.

10: Resources

Check For Names

KnowEm (http://knowem.com/) – Allows you to check for your name across different social media channels to see what is are available.

Sharing Widgets

AddThis (http://addthis.com) – Code snippets that you can use for free to offer sharing functionality on your website. They also have a Wordpress widget to eliminate the need for cutting and pasting code.

ShareThis (http://www.sharethis.com/) – Offers code snippets (including a Wordpress widget) that you can use for free to offer sharing functionality on your website. The difference between AddThis and ShareThis often depends on what style you prefer.

Graphic Design

Canva (https://www.canva.com/) – A free web app that makes it easy to create web graphics, like Facebook Cover images and graphic posts.

Fiverr (http://fiverr.com) – A freelance site where you can look for someone offering to design profile art for $5.

Pixlr (http://pixlr.com) – A powerful, free picture editor that offers similar functionality to Photoshop without the cost.

Posting To Social Media

Hootsuite (http://hootsuite.com) – Software you can use to schedule your social media posts in advance. They offer a free account for posting on up to five social media accounts.

10: Actionable Checklist

- What message do your profiles send (in the copy and visually) about your business?
- Have you filled out as many fields as possible in your profiles (especially your address and phone in Facebook)?
- In what ways are you reaching out to your current customers to connect with them through social media? Could you do more?
- Have you tried posting during the best times that we listed to see if it leads to better results?

[11]
How to Get Sales with Facebook

I LIKE YOU A LOT

Genuine Interest
Facebook is currently one of the giants of the social media world, and is becoming more and more relevant for businesses. If you don't have a page set up for your business yet, do it right now!

For the purposes of this section, we're going to assume that you have at least opened your business Facebook fan page.

It is important to build a fan base on Facebook so you can extend your marketing reach. In other words, you want to get as many interested people seeing your Facebook posts as possible.

Interested is the key.

There are many ways to beef up your fan base fast, including buying them. While that may make it look like you have a lot of fans, it can also be detrimental in the long run. Yes, you want to use Facebook to increase your reach, but you can actually reduce your chances of being seen if the fans you've acquired aren't really interested in what you have to say. Just because you're connected with someone doesn't mean that they will see what you post - that's all going to be determined by previous engagement.

Facebook tabulates how often you engage with posts from someone to determine where their activity (posts) is seen in your feed. For example, if Jerry is friends with Elaine and George, that doesn't mean he'll always see their posts. Say Jerry frequently Likes and comments on Elaine's posts, but never on George's. That tells Facebook that Jerry isn't that interested in George's posts, so they should be bumped to the bottom of his feed, or not shown at all. Jerry's just not that into George.

The same is true for a Facebook page. If the percentage of people that engage (Like, comment, click on, or share) on a post is small, then Facebook will stop showing it to people. The data is telling Facebook that people aren't interested in what you have to say, and that stinks for you and your business.

CONTESTS

Contests can be great ways to encourage engagement and acquire new fans. If you decide to run a contest to attract new fans, try to ensure that they're interested in your content by offering a prize that is tied to your offerings, maybe something like:
- Store credit
- A gift certificate
- A free product/service (that you sell)
- An invitation to a special event

There are plenty of Facebook apps that make it easy to run contests. They cost money, but fortunately most are very affordable since they have small businesses in mind.

Use Facebook contests to:
- Increase the number of Likes
- Get people to take polls (market research)
- Generate engagement (shares, Likes, comments)
- Source marketing assets that you can use for other things (pictures, videos)

Contest Ideas

Let's talk about some of the most common types of contests you can run to boost your Facebook following.

Sweepstakes – This is a contest where the winner is determined via a random drawing. Usually Facebook users enter the sweepstakes by Liking your page (if they aren't a fan already) and then filling out a form with their contact information. Many times sweepstakes offer bonus entries if someone shares the contest with their friends and then the friends enter (which really increases the number of participants and the engagement).

Remember what we said earlier, your prize should be something tied to your product/service. It doesn't necessarily have to be something you offer (although that's probably best), but it should at least be related. For instance, if you sell sporting goods, you may offer a new iPad (which is sure to lure people in), but it would be wiser to give tickets to a sporting event as a prize instead. The chances of a new Facebook fan being interested in your brand is much higher when you give away the tickets since you know that this person probably likes and/or plays sports.

Video or Picture Submission Contest – This is contest where people submit videos or pictures meeting specific criteria you establish. You can be the one to choose a winner or others can vote for the winner. If you choose the winner, you will be assured it's the one you like the best. On the other hand, when Facebook users vote, the contest can get a lot more traffic as submitters encourage their friends to visit the page and vote for them.

The method of selecting a winner can largely depend on what your primary goal is for the contest. If you're mainly trying to increase engagement or your fan base, it may make sense to entice entrants to bring more traffic (and vote for them) by allowing the users to select the winner. However, if your objective is to source assets that you can use in future marketing campaigns, you may want to handpick the winner. If you do have Facebook users select, think about including a clause that stipulates that you have the right overrule the users in certain circumstances. For example, you may not want to have a winner that includes inappropriate images/language in their material or openly disparages a competitor (which could lead you right into court).

Polls – Polls are a fun way to engage people or to conduct market research. Few and far between are the people that like to take polls or surveys, but when you offer an incentive like a prize, attitudes start to change. Using polls to conduct serious market research can expose things you can do to increase sales, something that is costly to do otherwise because of the difficulty in locating participants. Another option is just to have a fun survey that increases engagement and reminds people of your offerings. If you're a bakery, right around Thanksgiving you might ask people what their favorite pie is and have them vote for their favorite from the types that you sell.

Fangate (content/coupon) – While not a contest, fangates can be run with the same software and helps accomplish a similar goal. Fangates protect pages from being seen unless someone is a fan. Essentially, it's a way to protect your valuable lead incentive. Instead of submitting a form, the person must become a fan of your Facebook page to receive the lead incentive. After the person clicks the button to become a fan, they get access to a page where they can download or view content you promise them.

Facebook Ads

If you've used Facebook, you've no doubt seen the ads that line the right side of each web page (Sponsored posts), and occasionally intermingle in your feed as a *Suggested Post*. While ads can lead you to other websites, Facebook's sponsored posts are different. Some of the ads lead you to other sites, but many of them are meant to increase your engagement within Facebook.

For example, if you look at this example of a Facebook page, the ads on the right side are leading you to external websites. However, the *Suggested Post* by Optimizely is trying to get you to like their page, keeping you *inside* Facebook.

Make Money on the Internet | 217

Whether you direct people to your website or keep them on Facebook depends on your objective.

I'm Looking for an Immediate Sale

Option A: Keep Them in Facebook
While Facebook won't come out and say it, most digital marketers say that the cost per click (CPC) is cheaper if you keep people on the site.

Think about it – if someone clicks on the Like button in an ad or if they click on your title (which leads to your Facebook page), Facebook can continue to make money by showing more ads. However, if the user leaves Facebook, they may not return immediately, which means lost ad money for Facebook.

People are more likely to thumb through your content if it's on Facebook than if they are taken somewhere else. The difference is people's expectations. If someone is on Facebook, they aren't actively looking for something, but may click on an ad out of sheer curiosity. When a link leads them away from Facebook, it disrupts what they were doing (reading through posts or using a Facebook app).

Compare that to when someone sees an ad when they're doing a web search. When a person is doing a search on Google, they're actively looking for something and they expect to be taken to another site outside of Google (and their flow and expectations remain intact).

If you're looking for an immediate sale, create landing pages within Facebook on custom tabs using third party apps. Once they are set up, direct people to these custom tabs (instead of to your main Page) with Sponsored posts for a higher conversion rate. If you send them to your main Page, there's too much content to try to focus on and too many things for them to do (aside from purchasing from you). You need to point them to exactly where you want them; they can browse the rest of your Facebook pages once they're in.

Option B: Send Them to Your Site
Keeping someone on Facebook can limit options for what you show people. While there are many apps that allow you to create a store within your Facebook page, you're still lim-

ited in what you can do; you'll never be able to control the whole user experience because you're still operating within the confines of the social network. In these cases, make sure that you follow the first rule of paid Internet ads and keep the message that's shown in the Sponsored post consistent on the page they're taken to.

Build a Relationship
While all business owners would like an immediate sale, it's often not that easy - especially if a person isn't actively looking for you. If Joe stumbles upon your ad for tacos while he's reading his Facebook posts to see what his friends are up to, he may be willing to Like you, but unless he's hungry and it's convenient, his visit probably won't result in an immediate sale. He's just not in the mindset to buy from you... yet.

Facebook is a lot about the **soft sell**. If you're willing to share tidbits about things that may interest your consumer base and approach them as a friend, they're likely to accept the occasional plug for your product/service. However, if you go for the hard sell and ram promotions down their throats, you'll likely turn people away.

If you're unsuccessful with driving people towards immediate purchases on Facebook or your product/service isn't conducive, focus on building a relationship with your Facebook users. Assuming that you already tried to build your Facebook fans through other means, consider running ads.

While it might take awhile to pay off since there's no immediate sale, paid ads to build your fan base can be profitable. Your goal is to build a relationship with your fans by offering them content that interests and entertains them so they think of you whenever they think of your product/service. To build on our previous example, you want Joe to think of you every time he thinks of tacos, so in the future when he does have a craving (the "need"), you're the one he buys from.

Creating a Facebook Ad

After you have an idea of what you want to accomplish with your Facebook marketing, you can create an ad.

Here's an example of how to create one:

(1) After you've created a Facebook ad account, select *Create Ads* from the menu:

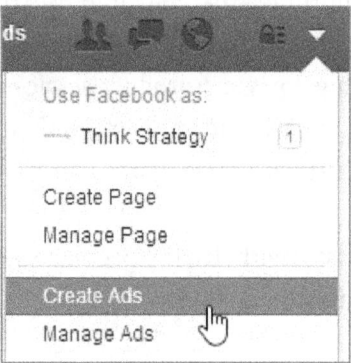

(2) This will take you to a screen that asks you what your objective is. In this example, we'll aim for increasing Page Likes:

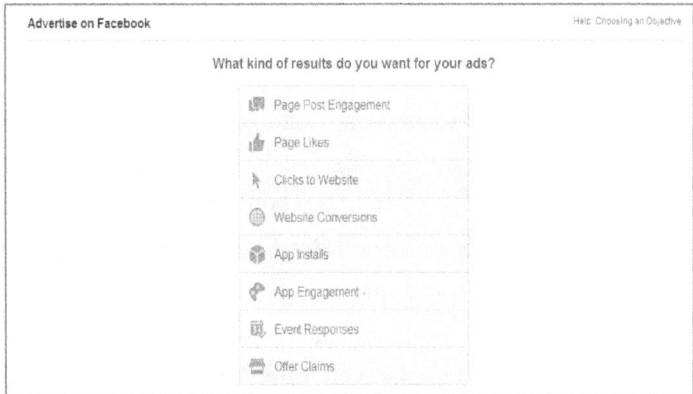

(3) After clicking *Page Likes*, you will select the page you want to create ads for based on which Pages you are a Manager for. After selecting the one you want, click *Continue*.

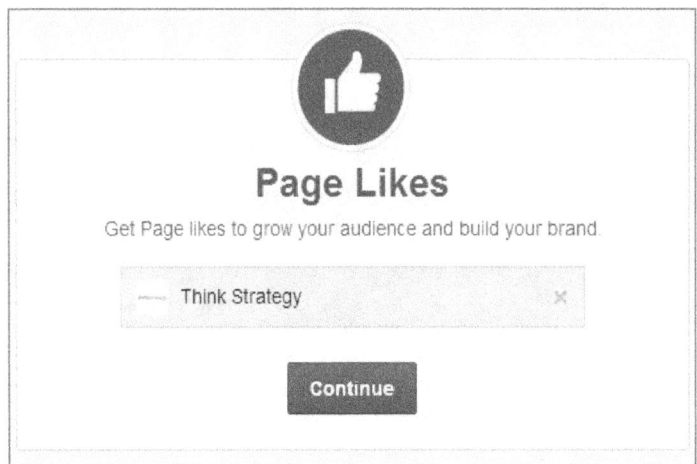

(4) On the next page, in the *Images* section, you can upload up to six different images (only one picture will be shown per ad). Facebook will rotate between these images when showing your ad.

Tips for Images:
- Upload multiple images so you can test which one gets the best results - the highest click-through rate, the highest percentage of conversions (Page Likes) and the lowest cost. After determining the image that gets the best results, you can stop the ads that are running for the images that didn't perform as well.
- Choose images that look good in multiple sizes because your ad may show in different sizes (you'll be able to preview the ads below).
- Choose images that get someone's attention, but don't be misleading. Nothing infuriates people more than clicking on an ad and not seeing what they expect.

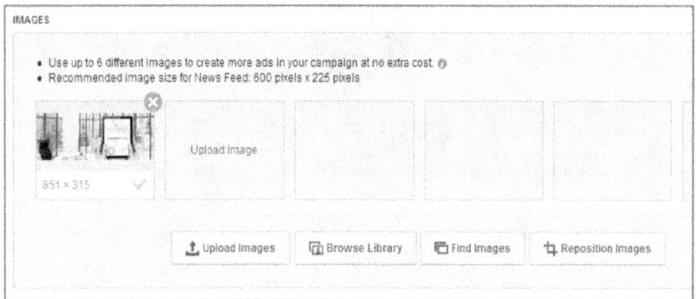

(5) In the *Text and Links* section, you'll be able to specify the text that shows with your ad and then preview what they'll look like.

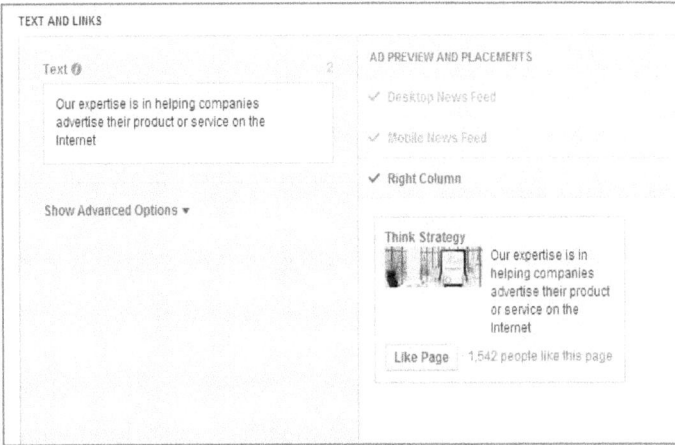

(6) The *Audience* section is what makes Facebook's advertising platform different than everyone else. You're able to specify whom you're targeting (your customer persona – remember that from the very beginning of this book?) because Facebook (a) knows who's viewing the ad because they are logged in and (b) they know about this user based on the user's settings (their profile, Likes, friends).

In this step, specify the following information to help better target your ad:

- **Locations** – Enter where your customers are located. If you leave it too broad, you may be wasting

your money because it will be unlikely that customers will see your ads.
- **Age** – How old your target market is (Again, don't leave it too broad. Are 13 year olds really likely to buy your product?).
- **Gender** – Does your customer base skew more toward one gender or another?
- **Language** – Limit it if your buyers speak one particular language.
- **More Demographics** – Click on this to specify even more about who your target customer is. One particularly useful setting for businesses that sell to specific industries is that "Work" section, where you can target based on the user's job title, employer or industry.

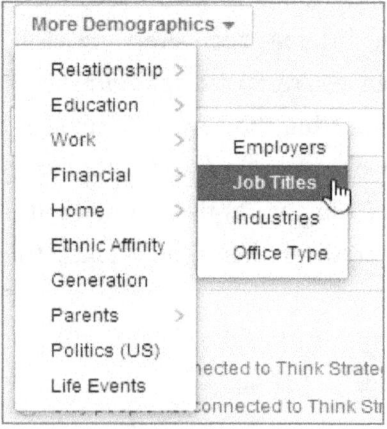

- **Interests** – Think of this field as indicating the kind of things that your target markets might like: competitors, publications/media that focus on what you sell, hobbies, etc.

- **Behaviors** – This field lets you target people based on something they've done in the past. For example, you could target based on whether this person has made a donation recently or made a certain type of purchase recently.

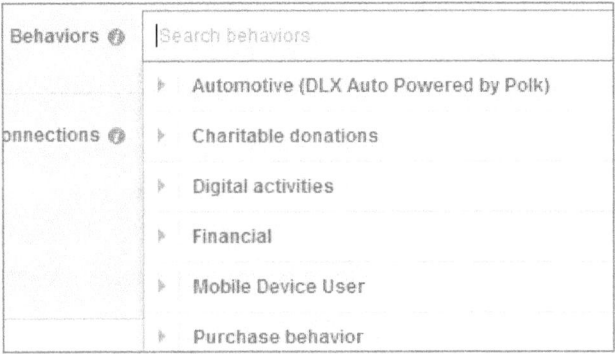

- **Connections** – Indicate if you want to target all users with this ad, users connected to you or only those who aren't connected to you (there are also additional advanced options to help further define this selection).

(7) In the *Campaign And Ad Set* section, enter a name for your campaign and ad set. Make sure it's something that is logical and makes sense to you. Also, set a daily budget and indicate a run schedule for your ads so Facebook knows when to stop showing your ads. You'll want to set a lower budget at first. Once you have at least a week to see how your ads perform, you can increase your spending budget.

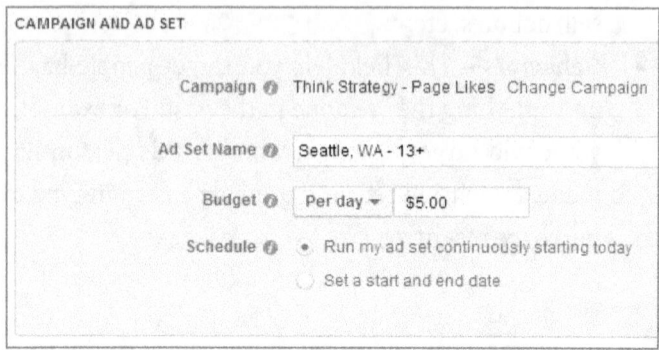

(8) In the *Bidding And Pricing* section, specify how much you want to bid for your ad running. You can choose to: Bid for clicks, Bid for impressions or *Bid for Page Likes*. We recommend *Bid for clicks* to start because it gives you the most control over the cost per conversion.

If you choose *Bid for clicks*, you can opt to manually set your cost per click (the amount you're charged any time someone clicks on your ad). Facebook will give you a suggested bid to start so you have some idea of where to begin. Review your ads daily and tweak this amount up or down based on the results of your ad campaign.

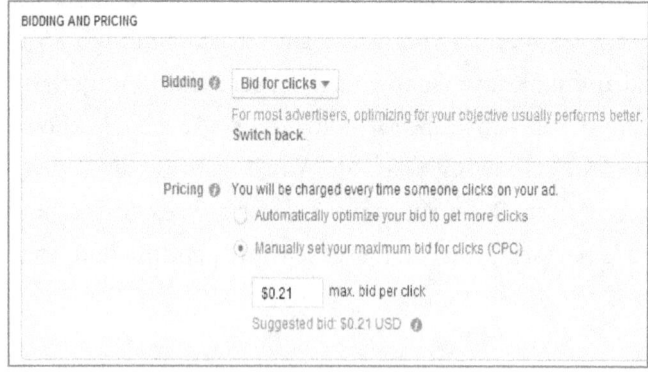

(9) After you've saved your ad, Facebook will review it and approve or reject the ad. If they reject it, they'll tell you why so you can make adjustments and resubmit the ad.

Managing a Facebook Ad
Once you create your ad campaign and it's approved, watch it closely so you can make adjustments. This is how you do it:

(1) You'll find a link in the Tools menu (look for the little down-arrow in your top navigation bar) for *Manage Ads*.

(2) There you'll see stats for your campaign (this is also where you can change the status to pause the whole campaign).

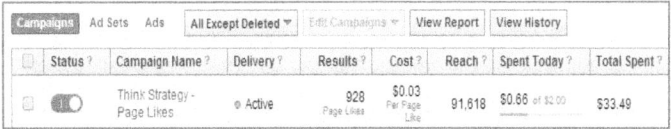

(3) Click on the tab for *Ads*.

(4) On this tab, you can see your ads' statistics:
- How many Likes you've received (this depends on the objective you chose)
- Your average cost per Like
- How many people have seen the ad ("Reach")
- How many times the average viewer has seen it ("Frequency")
- How many have clicked your ad (since you pay per click on the ad, not per Like)
- How often a viewer clicks on your ad ("Click-Through Rate")
- How much you've spent

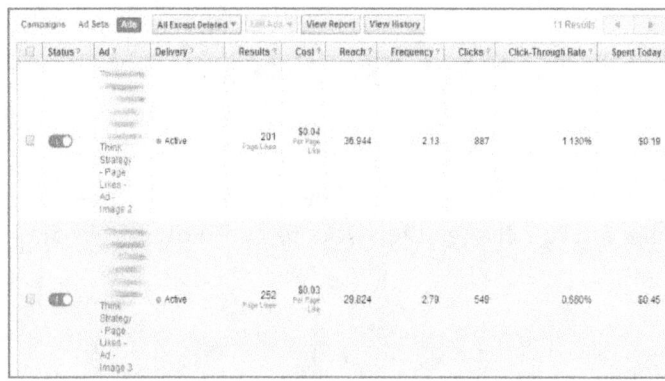

Depending on how your ads are performing, you may want to make changes.

- To stop an ad (make it inactive), click this icon to the left of your ad name:

- To edit an ad (change your target, your bid, etc.) click on the ad name, and then click on an *Edit Creative* link, like this one:

- If you're not getting enough clicks, consider raising your daily budget in the campaign settings (if you're hitting your daily limit) or an ad's *Bid Per Click* (you may not be getting shown enough if your bid is too low).

As a general rule, test lowering your *Bid Per Click* as your click-through rate rises because Facebook is likely to still show your ad if you bid a little less than others since visitors are still clicking on your ads. Facebook shows the ads to make money and even if someone bids a high amount for a click, it doesn't matter if visitors aren't clicking their ads.

No clicks = no money for Facebook.

Over time, stop the ads that don't work. This will happen eventually to all ads; people get ad fatigue. They just don't respond to an ad over time; they get sick of seeing it, they already clicked on it, the offer doesn't appeal to them any more, etc. If you start to see that your Cost Per Like ("Result" cost) is increasing, it's a sign that your ad needs to be replaced.

11: Resources

Contests

Wildfire (http://www.wildfireapp.com) - Wildfire (owned by Google) offers a social networking software suite that not only lets you run contests, but also post messages, run ads, create landing pages, and view analytics from one place.

Wishpond (http://wishpond.com) - Software that lets you run contests and place ads. It offers month-to-month pricing based on the features you want.

Woobox (http://woobox.com) - Software that lets you run a variety of contests and place Facebook ads. Offers month-to-month pricing based on how many Facebook fans you have.

Facebook Ads

Facebook Advertising (https://www.facebook.com/advertising) - Create your Facebook ad account to start running marketing campaigns on the site.

11: Actionable Checklist

- What message does your Facebook profile send (in the text and visually)?
- Are you going to push for the immediate sale or develop a relationship with visitors to your Facebook page?
- What strategy will you use to accomplish your Facebook objectives?
- Are you getting enough engagement from fans?
- Would it help increase engagement to run a Facebook contest?
- Have you tried advertising on Facebook (even with a daily budget of just $1)?
- Are you actively monitoring and adjusting your Facebook ad campaigns?

[12]

Become a Digital Pied Piper on Twitter

Twitter is another social media giant that you'll want to turn your attention to.

Twitter is a social media app that lets people share info via tweets, which are short messages made up 140 characters – letters, numbers, symbols – or less. As you might guess, to increase your reach on Twitter, you want to accumulate as many Followers as possible.

A notable difference between Twitter and Facebook is how they decide to show your posts in users' feeds. Facebook uses an algorithm that determines what posts to show to a user, in what order, based on previous engagement levels (i.e. how often posts resulted in actions from users - a click, Like, share, or comment). Twitter, on the other hand, shows all posts from people you follow in chronological order. This means that while it benefits you to attract followers that will engage with your tweets, engagement doesn't carry the same weight as it does on Facebook.

Grow Organically

Just like on your website, when you consistently share valuable, informative content on Twitter, you'll start to build up a following. People will start to stumble upon your posts as they search for topics. As new users find your tweets, they'll retweet your posts to their followers, and you'll attract more people to you.

To help people find your tweets, use **#hashtags** in your tweets (# + keyword/s) Hashtags are a way of communicating what your tweets are about and attracting views. They help tweets become part of a conversation that people can follow and join.

While hashtags help create a conversation, avoid the temptation of using too many hashtags because your tweets

#tend #to #start #looking #spammy #and #discourage #people #from #following #you. Try to limit yourself to no more than a couple of hashtags per tweet.

Tweets That Get the Most Engagement
Want to know what tweets receive the most engagement? Here it is straight from the horse's mouth - Twitter conducted its own survey and this is what they found[6] :
- Photos average a 35% boost in retweets.
- Videos get a 28% boost.
- Quotes get a 19% boost in retweets.
- Including a number receives a 17% bump in retweets.
- Hashtags receive a 16% boost.

Twitter did find that these results varied by industry, so your mileage may vary. To determine how the stats above impacts your tweet engagement, sign-up for a free Twitter Ads account (http://ads.twitter.com). In there you can view your tweet analytics to see what your audience responds to most:

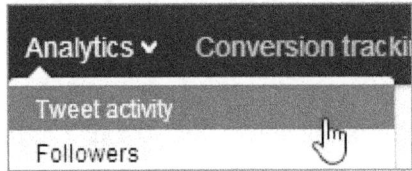

---

[6] Rogers, Simon. 10 March 2014. *What Fuels a Tweets Engagement?* Retrieved 16 June 2014, from https://blog.twitter.com/2014/what-fuels-a-tweets-engagement.

Join the Conversation

Something nice about Twitter is that you can see other users' tweets without being a follower of theirs (unless the user has their settings set so that only followers can see their tweets). That makes it easy to start up discussions with others. It takes some digging sometimes because of the sheer volume of tweets, but it's a good way to attract potential customers and build your follower base.

For example, let's say you're a law firm. You may run daily searches on "lawyer" to see if there are some conversations you get involved with. Here are some we found with that simple, broad search:

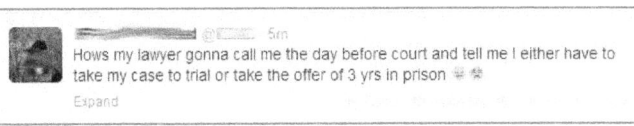

Just from a few tweets within ten minutes, you've found some people that may be prospects or people you might be able to interact with. Aside from maybe getting business from these people, by replying to them, you are now a part of a public conversation that others may see. This creates a multiplier effect where more people than just the original Tweeter become exposed to you and your offerings.

Follow You, Follow Me
One interesting behavior on Twitter is that if you follow someone, they will often follow you back.

Knowing this, one strategy a lot of Twitter users do is to follow others they think may be interested in their tweets. If you decide to use this technique, don't get too carried away; use it in moderation.

Twitter tries to stop users from going crazy by setting limits on how many users it thinks is reasonable to follow within a certain time frame (i.e. daily, weekly, etc.). When you hit that limit, Twitter will let you know and you'll have to slow down adding followers and/or drop some people that you follow. Try to follow a maximum of 100 users/day to stay under their thresholds.

There are several ways to find users to follow who are also interested in your tweets. One way that we already mentioned above is to do searches on Twitter and follow people who come up in the results that you think are a good fit based on what they tweet about.

Another way is to use a free tool like **Tweetpi**. Tweetpi will allow you to find users who may be interested in your tweets by showing followers of users you specify. For example, if you're a bookseller, you may want to target Goodreads followers because you know they're into reading.

In Tweetpi:

(1) Click on the link for *Follow followers*.

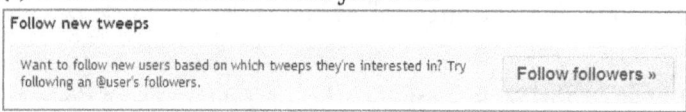

(2) On the next page, enter the username whose followers you're interested in seeing, preceded by "@," and then click the button for *Start following*.

Follow @user's followers

The simplest way to find and add people with the same interests as you on Twitter is to find a popular tweep under your topic, say 'phpc' or 'techcrunch' for the geeky people like myself, and add people that follow these known users or communities. (@user's friends instead?)

@goodreads

Start following »

(3) This will show you a list of users that follow the username you specified. From there, you can see different stats (which you can sort by), such as:

- How many people they follow
- Their follow ratio (how many people they follow compared to how many follow them)
- Their last tweet

You can also add or remove columns (to adjust the stats shown) by clicking on the *Columns* button:

Default Button (what's this?) : [icons] Columns ▼ ✖ Reset Sorting Options ▼

Premium Tools Lists: [icons] Default List [icons] Load/load Scores Skip previously followed or unfollowed?

Image	Screen Name	User Information			Tweep...
		Location	# follow...	Last Tweet *	Follow Ratio
	hannahlatt [Follow]	Buffalo, NY	475	about 4 hours ago	45%
	JoeLarson111 [Follow]	N 35°13' 0" / W 80°52' 0"	357	about 1 month ago	43%
	Arleta1 [Follow]	Caerphilly	268	about 8 hours ago	78%
	DameEmma [Follow]	Canada	214	18 days ago	54%
	kaatee24 [Follow]		200	18 minutes ago	36%

240

From this screen, you can click the Follow button to become a follower.

Tweetpi offers a lot of other useful features, including the ability to follow the same people as other users (which could be a good way of targeting people interested in your products/services).

Aside from attracting the user you just followed to be a follower, you may also appeal to some of the people that follow them.

One common thing that users will do to attract retweets is to tweet the names of users they followed recently, such as this:

Which in turn lead to a retweet with more users being exposed to our Twitter account.

Enhancing Your Follows

One thing that some users do to enhance the experience of following is to send a direct message to new followers. Using a tool such as **justunfollow**, you can automatically send a message whenever you receive a new follower. Be forewarned though: not all people will be receptive to your direct message, so it could lead to some unfollows. This is especially true if your direct message is perceived to be spammy.

If you want to automate sending a direct message in justunfollow:

(1) After you sign-up and login, click the *Automate* link on the left menu:

(2) On the next screen, check the box for *Automatically send welcome **Direct Message** to new followers*:

(3) Type the message new followers will receive in the text box:

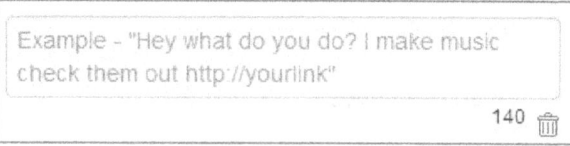

(4) Click the Save button.

New followers will now receive an automated direct message like this (you can remove the justunfollow.com portion by paying for a subscription):

Lead Generation Cards

Lead generation cards are a feature that Twitter created to help businesses get more leads from the social media site. Instead of trying to direct viewers to a landing page to get a lead incentive, they can click a button (which gives you their email address from their Twitter card). The card attaches to the bottom of a tweet like this:

When the user clicks *Download Now*, they're directed to where they can get the free guide and their email address is sent to you.

Creating Cards

To create a card, you have to first start a free Twitter Ads account. After getting your account set-up, here's what you do:

(1) Select *Creatives > Cards* from the top menu:

(2) On the Cards Manager screen, select whether you want to create a **Lead Generation card** or a **Website card**:

- **Lead Generation cards** are meant to capture the person's email address so you can contact them as a potential lead.
- **Website cards** tell about your Website and are meant to drive more traffic to it.

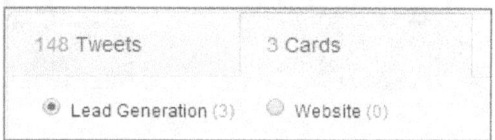

(3) For a Lead Generation card, the first field to complete is your **short description** – this will show as a short, bold headline (most likely the first thing viewers read) that will tell someone why they should give you their contact details:

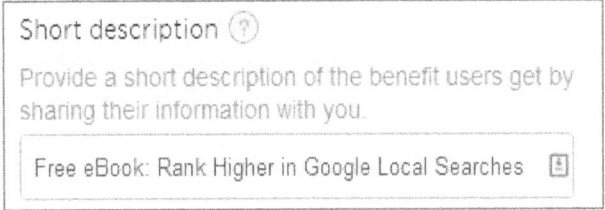

(4) Next, upload an image. Make sure that your image meets the minimum requirements otherwise Twitter won't allow the upload:

(5) In the *Call to action* field, let viewers know what they should do:

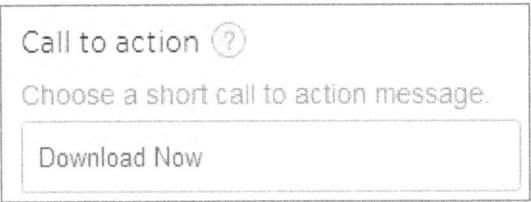

(6) Enter the URL to your privacy policy so people have an understanding what you might do with their contact information and how many have access to it:

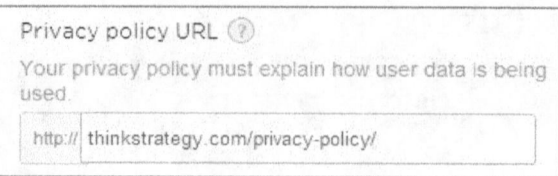

(7) In the *Destination URL* field, provide the place where you want users to go after they give you their contact info:

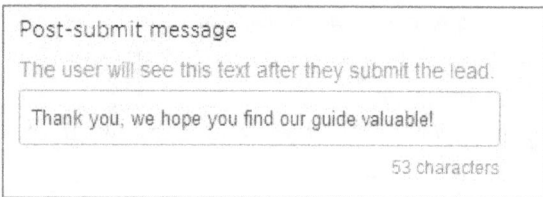

(8) Enter a message that users will see after they submit their info:

(9) Name your card:

Make Money on the Internet | 247

(10) Read the Terms and Conditions and mark the checkbox if you agree (if you don't agree, you won't be able to continue):

(11) Click Create card to save your new card:

Using Your Cards

After you create your cards, it's time start generating leads. To use your Lead Generation cards, log into your Twitter Ads account.

(1) Select *Creatives > Cards* from the top menu:

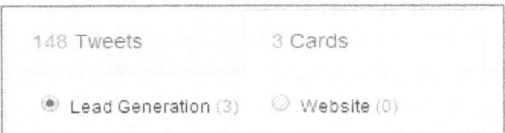

(2) Select whether the card you want to attach is a Lead Generation or Website one:

(3) Place your mouse over the card you want to use, and then click this icon:

(4) In the *New Tweet* pop-up box that appears, type your message before the URL of your card:

(5) Click the *Tweet* button.

Congratulations, you've now created your first Twitter lead generation system!

Your new tweet will function like a normal one, except this one will have the picture you uploaded, the headline you wrote, and the button that will trigger their contact information being sent to you (and direct them to where they can get your lead incentive).

Getting started with Twitter is fast and easy and can be done on a very limited budget, so it's another tool to build into your overall marketing plan.

12: Resources

Twitter Tools

Hashtag.org (http://hashtag.org) – A website that lists popular hashtags on Twitter and can give you ideas on content that people may be interested in reading about.

Tweetpi (http://tweetpi.com) – Tweetpi can give you ideas for Twitter users who may be interested in following you. Use this free tool to get suggestions on people you can follow.

Twitter Ads (http://ads.twitter.com) – A free tool filled with Twitter analytics which will show you what tweets are getting the highest engagement levels and can be used to create Lead Generation cards. It can also be used to run paid campaigns to attract more traffic to your tweets and profile.

Justunfollow (http://www.justunfollow.com) – Use it to automatically send direct messages to new followers for free; to welcome them and reinforce what they can expect from your Twitter posts.

12: Actionable Checklist

- Have you set up your Twitter profile and filled it out completely?
- Have you started organically building your follower base?
- Have you signed up for Twitter Ads?
- Have you reviewed your Analytics in Twitter Ads so you know what's getting you the most engagement?
- Have you tried adjusting some of your tweets to include details that Twitter says increases engagement and measured if that helped in Twitter Ads' Analytics?
- Have you tried Twitter's Lead Generation or Website cards?

[13]

Link In to Business to Business (B2B) Leads

While most people recognize LinkedIn as a great place to network with other professionals and to look for and get jobs, many haven't considered the power it has to land B2B leads. Since people generally list their job title and employer in their profiles, it's easy to target people who fit your customer persona. Also, you can bet that LinkedIn data is probably more accurate than other social media sites since the function is more professional than social.

Image Is Everything

Similar to other social media sites, your profile on LinkedIn is important. Since LinkedIn has a more business-y feel than the other sites, you will want to keep your profile more conservative. That doesn't mean it has to be stuffy, just more business-focused. It's ok to reflect the nature and culture of your business and show your personality. After all, people buy from other people, not from a nameless business. The expectation is that viewers will learn about your credentials when viewing your profile, and talking about qualifications is no joking matter!

It all starts with your profile picture – the first thing that someone will see when searching for your profile. This means that instead of a selfie at the beach, go with a profile picture that is more fitting your profession – so either in appropriate business attire or your uniform. Show people that you're going to deliver when they're your customer.

Next, you want to fill in as many fields in your profile as possible. The more complete, the more your customers or potential customers will learn about you.

Once your profile is complete, start to connect with as many people in your professional network as you can on LinkedIn, so others can see how entrenched you are in your industry. This is where you can start to leverage the real power of this social network.

Use Endorsements to Show You Have The Skills

Aside from filling out the profile settings thoroughly, you

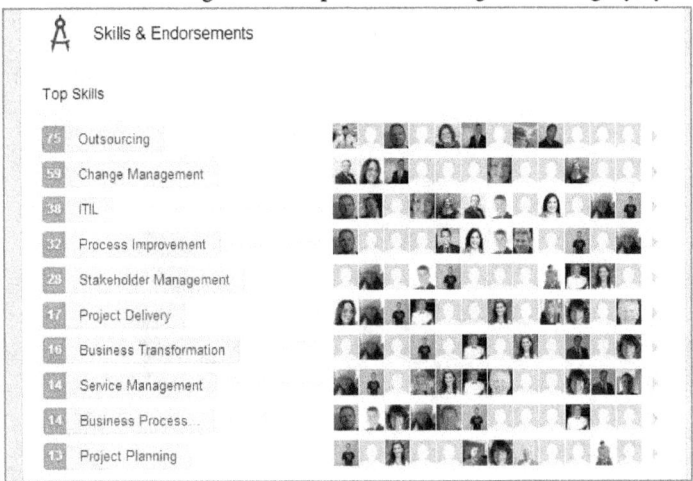

have to work on LinkedIn to demonstrate your credibility. First, you want to get people to "Endorse" you for specific skills that you have. This gives people confidence that you have these skills necessary for the work you want to perform for them.

LinkedIn makes it easy to endorse one of your connections. To give an endorsement, go to the profile page for that person.

(1) Click the *"Endorse"* button that's near the top of the person's profile.

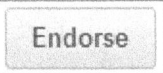

(2) A blue box will display above the person's profile. In it will be the skills already attributed to them. You can then:

- Remove a skill from your endorsement by clicking the small "x" next to the skill.
- Add another skill you want to endorse the person for by typing it in the white box.

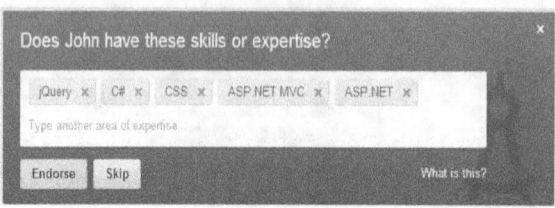

(3) Click *Endorse*.

To receive endorsements from other people, send him or her a note and ask if they'll give you one. Another technique is to endorse people who you'd like to return the favor. Whenever you endorse someone, they are notified and prompted to return an endorsement back to you.

Testimonials, the LinkedIn Way

Testimonials are not only a way to build your credibility on your website, but also on LinkedIn. On LinkedIn, they're called "Recommendations" and by default are displayed near the bottom of your profile. You do have the option to move them higher up in your profile, which is something we recommend doing.

Make Money on the Internet | 257

To give a recommendation to another LinkedIn member, you'll have to provide some basic information beyond the actual recommendation. LinkedIn takes these very seriously and wants to ensure that you have an actual professional relationship with the person you're recommending.

To begin, first go to their profile page.

(1) Find the **Recommendations** section in their profile. You may need to scroll down a bit to find it.

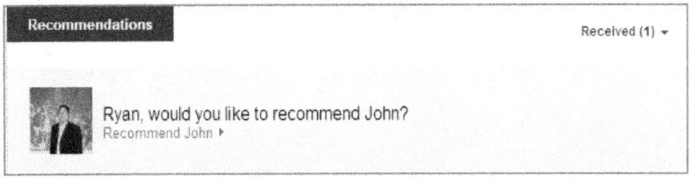

(2) Click the blue link for **Recommend [person's name].**

(3) Indicate how you know this person (Colleague, Service Provider, Business Partner, Student).

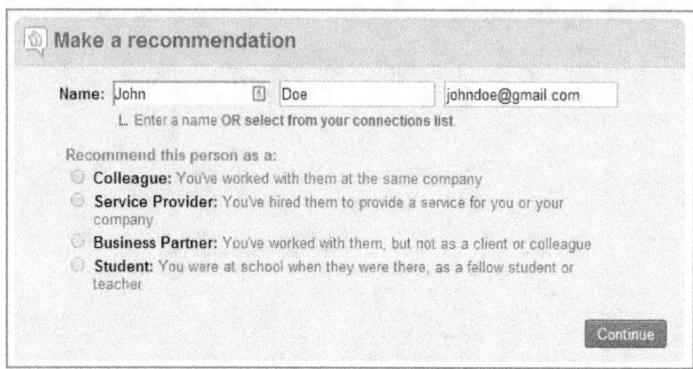

(4) On the next screen you will provide your actual recommendation.

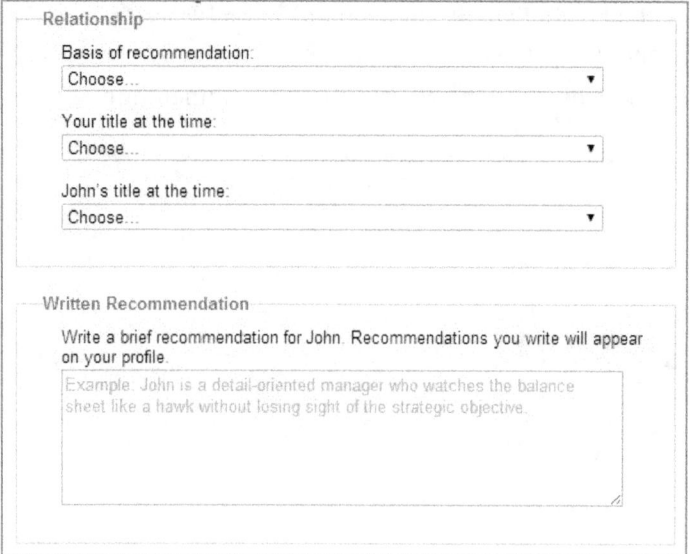

(5) Click *Send* to submit your recommendation.

Similar to endorsements, you can encourage people to leave recommendations for you by asking for them or providing one first.

PROSPECTING

Since you already know the occupation of your target customer persona(s), you can now search for them on LinkedIn. However, you won't always be able to message them directly to connect. Some people limit who can message them directly, so unless you already have some sort of connection with them (LinkedIn asks for "proof" in the form of your needing to enter their email address and indicate how you know them), you may need to use a paid service.

To search for prospects on LinkedIn:

(1) Enter the job title of your customer persona in the Search field at the top of the page and click the magnifying glass icon:

(2) Once the results appear, filter them using the options in the far left column. Some of the options are only available for paid subscribers, but many useful ones are available for free.

Once you find a good prospect, you can then send them an InMail (LinkedIn's name for direct messages on the site) if you're connected to them, are in a group with them or subscribe to a paid plan.

When you're sending a message and it's going to be out of the blue for the recipient (they don't know you and are not expecting your message), make sure that this first message isn't too long, it's not a sales pitch right off the bat and you tell them something that intrigues them. Just make it a brief introduction letting them know what pain points you can address for them or maybe something you could provide to them for free (i.e. consultation, analysis, white paper, etc.). Remember, you're just trying to start a conversation with them. Test out different message points in different InMail messages and see what people respond to the most.

GETTING YOUR GROUP ON

Being active in groups helps you develop a positive reputation on LinkedIn, and as a side benefit, it allows you to message people whom you couldn't ordinarily. If you go to a profile of someone whom you don't have a connection (and they aren't in a group with you), you'll see just a *Connect* button:

However, if you view the profile of someone *in a group you belong to,* even if you don't have a connection, you'll see the option for sending them an InMail (a message). Immedi-

ately, your options open up just because you're in the same group.

To find a group that you'd like to join:

(1) Enter a description of the type of groups you're interested in in the *Search* bar at the top of the page.

Some ideas might be:
- Use the job title of your prospects
- Use your job title
- The name of your industry
- Your geographical area

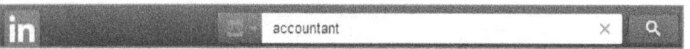

(2) Select the Groups link on the left to limit the results to only groups:

(3) From the results, click on the title of a group you're interested in:

Business Control for Finance/ Controller/ Controlling/ Management **Accountant**/ Accounting Prof.
Become a member to expand your network, boost... / Management **Accountant**/ Accounting Professionals.
Very Active: 162 discussions this month · 72,536 members
› 36 in your network · Similar

(4) If you look around and think the group is a good match, then click the *Join* button. Depending on the settings of the group, you may be automatically accepted as a member, or you may need to be manually approved/added by the group moderator.

Once you're in a group, you'll be able to make posts and comment on other posts in the group.

Post things that are informative and relevant to the group. Most groups have policies that they don't accept spam. The moderator can kick you out for this and LinkedIn may also mark all of your posts as needing manual approval before appearing in the group if enough people flag your posts as inappropriate.

Avoid making posts that are just sales pitches. Yes, we all think that we have the latest and greatest thing, especially when we're having a sale, but most people are immediately turned off when they see such an overt sales pitch when they're not expecting it. This, in turn, makes them angry and they may flag your message as inappropriate.

Make sure that the comments you share are valuable. Avoid writing ones like the example below where there is no substance. In this case, simply Liking the post would be appropriate. If you agree or disagree at least take the time to explain why you agree or which points of the post you felt most strongly about.

If you're able to be consistent with your posting and comments daily in the group, then your group reputation will grow. In fact, you can reach a point where you are a "Top Contributor" and your posts gain a higher visibility in the group, and that rank is also noted under your name and in the right hand column of the page.

Ask To Be Introduced

Sometimes you may find someone on LinkedIn that you'd like to communicate with, but they're not in one of your groups and you aren't connected with them. In such cases, you can sometimes ask a friend to introduce you if you have a mutual acquaintance.

To do this, go to the profile of the person you want to connect with, and then select *Connect > Get introduced* (which will show if you have shared connections).

If you do have a shared connection, you can then send a message to your connection asking that they introduce you.

Paying To Know You

Sometimes you want to message someone but LinkedIn won't let you because you're not in a group with them and you have no connection. In that case, you may want to consider a LinkedIn paid membership (like LinkedIn Premium), such as their ones for sales professionals. You still won't be able to contact everyone on LinkedIn (they must be in your 1st, 2nd, or 3rd degree network), but it can increase your reach by 35x.

With paid memberships you can send InMails to more people, but you have a limited number per month that you can send. Based on the level of plan you're on, you have a set number of credits, like 10, that you get for the month. Each time you write an InMail to someone who you don't already have a connection with, one credit will be deducted. The good news is that LinkedIn has a response guarantee, which means that if you don't get a response within seven days of sending an InMail, they refund your credit that you can then use to send a message to someone else.

Aside from paid memberships, you can also use LinkedIn's ad platform to reach potential customers. It works similar to the way it is on other social media platforms. You simply create an ad campaign targeted to your customer persona's job title(s) and point it to a landing page. This works a little differently than paid memberships because instead of you initiating the contact, the potential customer must reach out to you by clicking on your ad (and filling out a form on a landing page you direct them to). The good part about LinkedIn ads is you don't pay unless someone has an interest and clicks on your ad.

13: Resources

LinkedIn Tools

LinkedIn Ads (https://www.linkedin.com/ads) – Run pay-per-click ads that show to your target market and drive traffic to a landing page selling your product or capturing leads.

LinkedIn Premium (https://www.linkedin.com/static?key=welcome_premium) – Upgrade your basic LinkedIn account so you can connect with more people and have additional filtering options in searches to better target your ideal customers.

13: Actionable Checklist

- Are all of your major skills listed in your LinkedIn profile?
- Is your LinkedIn Profile as complete as possible?
- Could you get more endorsements from your connections for skills?
- Do the recommendations you have speak to all of the major traits you'd like to emphasize?
- Can you get more recommendations?
- Are there more groups you can join so you're exposed to more potential customers?
- Have you tried reaching out to some prospects using InMail and tested different messages to see which one(s) gets the best results?

[14]

Generate Demand with Pictures on Instagram & Pinterest

We've just focused on three of the biggest social media networks that you can use for your business, but now let's turn to two more up and comers that are becoming big players not just for personal entertainment and expression, but for businesses, as well.

Instagram and Pinterest are two social media sites that are picture or image-based and are great tools for generating leads and sales for businesses.

By sharing images, you create interest in your products and services and build your fan base. Those fans can then be converted to customers. If you sell products, pictures are a great way to draw interest to what you're selling – you can showcase new products to generate excitement, even offering "exclusive sneak peeks" to new products. Post pictures of real people using your products to give customers ideas how they might also find the item valuable; it allows them to imagine themselves using or wearing your product.

Even if you're not selling a product that is visually stimulating, challenge yourself and your team to come up with interesting ways to draw a lot of attention to your business. This is a perfect opportunity to get creative and showcase your brand personality. You can post images that are just meant to grab people's attention and then place text on top of the image - there doesn't necessarily have to be a correlation between the image you choose and what you sell (you don't need any fancy photo editing software or skills, there are tons of free or inexpensive alternatives that you can use to enhance and add text to your pictures).

Similar to other social networks, a great deal of your success will depend on how many followers you have on both Pinterest and Instagram.

Use Quality Images That Wake Up Emotions

On both Instagram and Pinterest (well, any social media site but these in particular), share images that are visually appealing and that immediately strike an emotional chord with people or make them think. You want them to be interesting. If you think the pictures are boring, how can you expect them to resonate with your followers? If you use images that you think are compelling and interesting, your passion will come across to others.

A lot of times humorous images catch people's attention and are shared with others who they'd like to make laugh. Aside from the image, you can add a funny caption in large text over the photo to make it entertaining (using a free tool like Canva). Make sure you're staying within the bounds of good taste and appropriateness – remember, you're representing your professional brand. Of course you want to make people laugh, but you still have to be cognizant of the fact that whatever you post *must* be reflective of your brand.

One misconception is that service providers are not a good fit for Instagram or Pinterest because they have no physical products to photograph. For example, if you're a law firm or accounting firm, you can still build an audience while promoting a professional and trustworthy image. How? Take high quality pictures around the office, of employees of the firm or items that project integrity (like professional books). If you have a particular niche, you can have images of the type of people that you serve. Make sure that your images are high quality pictures so you maintain the professional image you want to project. Here are just a few of the images we found when we searched for #lawyer on Instagram:

Give Credit Where Credit Is Due

Where can you find photographs or graphic images to use on Instagram or Pinterest?

You don't have to be a graphic designer or expert photographer to find great images to share. Of course if you can use your own photos and images, that's awesome and probably the easiest way. But what if your photos always have the edge of your finger in them and you want something a little more polished?

The good news is there are tons of great resources online where you can find really top-notch photos and images to use, many for free or at a very low cost. There are some sites where you either have to pay per image or purchase credits that you use to buy images, but there are so many great ones where you don't have to pay anything. Your best place to start is, of course, Google. Search for something like "free images" or "free [insert your industry] images." If you want a very specific image but can't get it yourself, you can "commission" a photographer to take a photograph for you on a site like Snapwire.

If you're not using your own images but instead ones you find on a stock image site or even on Flickr or PhotoPin, **make sure you read and understand the licensing rights.** Some sites are very liberal with how you can use images found on their site, others are very strict and even include information about altering or editing the original. Make sure they have some sort of Commercial Commons use. Most times, you at least need to give credit to the originator. It's easy to do – either in an accompanying caption or in the text or as an overlay on the photo (using a tool like Canva). But don't open yourself up to trouble – give proper attribution. Some sites, iStock for instance, have very stiff monetary penalties if you are caught using an image that you didn't obtain properly.

Don't worry about being literal with your images. Sometimes you may want to convey a certain emotion or feeling, or perhaps use an image in an unexpected way. This is a wonderful time to open up your mind and let your creativity flow.

This brings up one more caution. Refrain from using images you find doing a general Google Images search. While you may find a treasure trove of great ones to use, you have no easy way of knowing where the image originated. You need to do a little more investigating to find the original and then verify the usage rights.

Your best and safest bet is to use your own images or ones owned by your business. It's super easy these days to take great photos, do some fancy editing using simple online tools or apps, add text and borders and post away!

Finally, if you're using customers or people in your photos, make sure you have their permission to use their likeness in your photos. Again, you don't want anyone to have any surprises when they're looking through your Pinterest or Instagram pages and see themselves in a photograph and didn't know about it.

INFOGRAPHICS

Pinterest can be a great place to share infographics. Infographics have been around for many years and are fun graphics that share statistics, trends and other useful information about topics, in a visual way. In exchange for making the graphic interesting, you attract people who wouldn't normally read (or even visit) a long article that contains information on why people need a service you provide. They're an effective way to present what might otherwise be boring information in a very engaging way.

While infographics used to be very work intensive to design, due to their rising popularity, there are now many software tools and apps you can use to create them that are free or inexpensive. Once again, Google is your go-to to find the resource that works best for you. Some of our favorites are Piktochart, Easel.ly, Venngage, and Visual.ly.

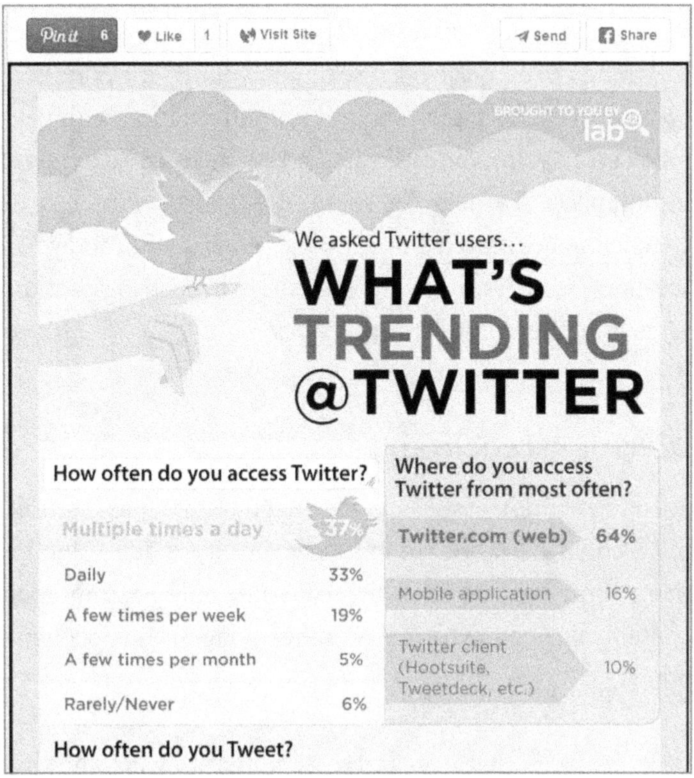

Make Money on the Internet | 279

| Pin it | 6 | ♥ Like | 1 | 👁 Visit Site | | ◀ Send | ▌Share |

We asked Twitter users...
WHAT'S TRENDING @TWITTER

BROUGHT TO YOU BY lab

How often do you access Twitter?

Multiple times a day	37%
Daily	33%
A few times per week	19%
A few times per month	5%
Rarely/Never	6%

Where do you access Twitter from most often?

Twitter.com (web)	64%
Mobile application	16%
Twitter client (Hootsuite, Tweetdeck, etc.)	10%

How often do you Tweet?

You can use infographics to illustrate trends in your industry, trends that you've been seeing in your own business or even to share resources and general information with your followers. Again, you're limited by your imagination with infographics. To help get some ideas, run a Pinterest or Google Images search on your topic *[+ infographic]* and you'll see how businesses have been using them to draw more eyeballs to their products or services.

Develop Relationships

Social networking is just as much about giving as it is taking. People are more apt to follow you if you add value for them somehow. Often that means not only posting good content, but commenting on other images and following others.

Look for users that have interests similar to yours and follow them. Then be sure to pay attention to what they're posting and provide honest, useful comments in return.

You can also look for people who are likely to give you exposure by seeing who does #shoutouts.

Engage Your Audience

Social networking is a dialogue, not a dictation. It's a conversation. Engage your audience by getting them involved and more invested in you and what you post. Some simple ways to do this are by posting questions along with your images (or written on them) or by holding contests.

Have contests to see:
- Who can come up with the best caption for a picture you post
- See which of your followers can post the best picture relevant to a theme you propose
- Who can get the most people to Like a photo that they post relevant to your business

The key is to make it fun!

Just recently, Pinterest launched their **Pinterest Analytics Tool** to make it easier for businesses to determine how their efforts on the social media site are paying off. This is a huge recognition of how effective a channel it is for businesses and how businesses that have a Pinterest presence can gain a real advantage over their competitors.

Businesses on Pinterest used to only know some basic stats about their pins, but not much beyond that – no real intelligence that they could use. With this more robust iteration, businesses can learn about actions that come from their boards. From this information you are able to determine where to spend your time and efforts most effectively – to get the biggest bang for each pin. You will gain analytics about your profile, your audience and activity from your website. Let's look at each of the three groupings:

- **Your Profile** – Here you will see the activity by Impressions, Repins, Clicks, and All-Time activity. You'll learn what are your most repined pins, ones that rank the highest, what gets seen the most, and what is opened. You can use this data to identify your most popular pins to repost to other boards, thereby extending your reach.
- **Your Audience** – Here you get to learn some valuable insight into your audience – more than just their demographics. You get to learn their interests and how they are interacting with your pins. You can filter the reports to see either the entire audience of Pinterest or just your followers. Look at both and compare the results to any goals you have set up for your Pinterest efforts. Here's the best part about this section – you can actually see what brands your followers are following, giving you a way to keep an eye on your competition.
- **Activity From (Your Website)** – In this section of your analytics, you'll see what people are pinning from your website. You'll learn what topics, images and pages from your site are striking a chord with your visitors.

So the first thing you should do when you get on Pinterest is make sure you set up your Pinterest business account so you don't miss a single pin!

14: RESOURCES

INFOGRAPHICS

These are tools to help you create fun infographics to draw attention to important information and stats on why people need your products/services.

Easel.ly (http://www.easel.ly)

Infogr.am (http://infogr.am)

Piktochart (http://piktochart.com)

Venngage (https://venngage.com)

Visme (http://www.visme.co)

CREATE YOUR OWN DESIGNS

Canva (http://www.canva.com) – This is a great site where you can create all sorts of images – from social media posts, cover images, blog graphics, headers, and more. Choose from their free components or pay only $1 for each premium element you select.

FINDING IMAGES TO USE

The following list is just a sampling of places you can search to find just the right image for your posts. Before using any images or photographs (in any way – for social media, your website or marketing materials), be sure to completely read and understand their terms and conditions of use. Look for Creative Commons licensing. You can find more by conducting a Creative Commons search on your favorite web browser, or by searching for things like "free stock images" [industry or topic].

Free Digital Photos (http://www.freedigitalphotos.net)

Free Images (formerly SXC) (http://www.freeimages.com)

MorgueFile (http://www.morguefile.com)

Unsplash (https://unsplash.com)

Big Stock Photo (https://www.bigstockphoto.com)

Flickr (https://www.flickr.com)

Free Media Goo (http://freemediagoo.com)

Dreamstime (http://www.dreamstime.com)

iStock (http://www.istockphoto.com)

Snapwire – (https://www.snapwi.re) - Buyers post a request for a specific photograph and a pool of photographers will respond by submitting their best work. You pay for the photo you like best.

14: Actionable Checklist

- Have you considered creating and posting infographics to Pinterest?
- Do you have any stats or facts that you could share via an infographic that could sway a viewer to become a buyer?
- Do you regularly look for other users (whom you may not know) that you could build a relationship with on Pinterest and Instagram?
- How can you increase engagement on Instagram and Pinterest?
- Have you started to build a library of photos from your business that you can use in your social media posts?

Part Four

Putting It Together & Driving Sales

[15]

Driving Sales with Search Engine Marketing

Although people see the ads all of the time, many businesses haven't tried search engine marketing or have tried it only to have limited success at it.

Search engine marketing (SEM) ads have three HUGE benefits not offered by other forms of media channels: (1) they're shown based on what the person searched for, so you know they're probably looking for this, (2) you only pay for the ad if someone clicks on it and (3) you can track what with the person did (if you installed Google Analytics and set-up your goals) to see your ROI. Compare that to advertising on TV, in print, on signage, or over the radio where:

- You're not sure how many people saw/heard your ad.
- You don't know the exact amount of sales the ad resulted in
- You're paying the same amount whether the viewer/listener was interested in hearing about your product/service or not
- You're advertising to people who aren't actively looking for your product/service at the time they come across your ad

That's not to say that advertising through other venues isn't without merits. For example, if you have a product/service that's extremely unique or new, people may rarely, if ever, search for it. Also, if you have enough money to run branding campaigns and want maximum exposure, it can be good to have more of a "shotgun" approach where you're hitting a much broader spectrum of people.

However, in terms of return on investment (ROI), SEM can be hard to beat.

You can test SEM with an extremely small budget, see the results and make changes in real-time. Once you've honed your ads and realized success in your tests, you can ramp up your spending or lower it whenever you want.

Pay-per-click ads are shown at the top and to the right of search results in Google and Bing.

Here are the results from a Google search on "hammer," with everything in red boxes representing paid ads:

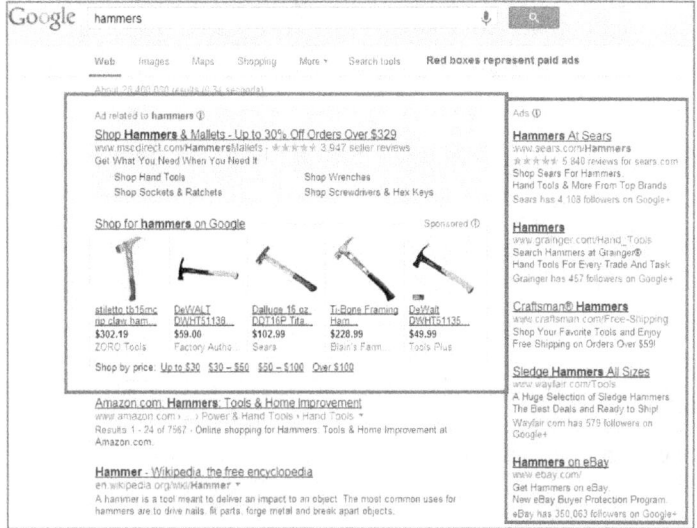

If you're interested in SEM, start with Google and Bing (they also run Yahoo's ads), the two largest search engines. Aside from search results, Google also places their ads on other websites and share the advertising revenue with the site.

SELECTING KEYWORDS

Earlier, we went over how to come up with the best keywords for your business/product/service, but that was just the start for SEM campaigns. With SEM, you'll always be revising your keywords as your results diminish or they get too expensive. Nothing lasts forever, and competitors' will eventually try to copy the keywords you're bidding on once they realize you're having success.

After you create your Google AdWords account, you create marketing campaigns where you specify which ads to show and what keywords you want to target. There are different factors to determine if your ad will appear or not. Aside from whether your keyword is related to the content or search results, another factor is how much you're bidding for a click. You can set the maximum bid amount at the campaign level so all keywords have the same price ceiling, or you can set the price at the keyword level.

Long Tail Keywords
Obviously, the higher you bid, the more likely your ad is to show in someone's search results. The most obvious keywords usually cost more because there's more competition for them (the tools provided by Bing and Google give you an idea of how much others are bidding for words).

PPC **long tail keywords** are a great way to help you get traffic through lower bids. Having a long tail means that the keywords are longer (there are more words) and more descriptive. For example, if "hammers" costs too much, try to add some other adjectives:

- [color] hammers (i.e. light blue hammers)
- [location] hammers (i.e. Seattle hammers)

- [adjective] hammers (i.e. low impact hammers, inexpensive hammers)

It takes more time to come up with lists like these (and you could end up with thousands of keywords), but it can dramatically lower your PPC bids. This is because they are time consuming to think of, so fewer people do it and competition drops off.

Long tail keywords get less traffic though, so you have to use more of them to compensate for the low level of traffic by having a lot of keywords.

Match Types
It's impossible to think about every conceivable keyword that someone will type. Keywords typed into search engines can run the gamut based on the question someone has on their mind. Think about it, how often do you describe something or ask a question with the same exact words as another person? Also, just think about the typos and the misspellings that people enter in a Google search.

The search engines account for these things by using match types. Match types allow search engines to look at your keywords more broadly, therefore showing for more searches than just the words you specified (unless you want it to be that strict).

To indicate the match type you want the search engine to use when determining if your keywords should be interpreted more broadly, you preface the keywords with symbols. Here's the example from Google:

Match type	Special symbol	Example keyword	Ads may show on searches that	Example searches
Broad match	none	Women's hats	include misspellings, synonyms, related searches, and other relevant variations	buy ladies hats
Broad match modifier	+keyword	+women's +hats	contain the modified term (or close variations, but not synonyms), in any order	hats for women
Phrase match	"keyword"	"women's hats"	are a phrase, and close variations of that phrase	buy women's hats
Negative match	-keyword	-women	are searches without the term	baseball hats

Creating Ads & Ad Groups

Once you determine the keywords you want to try, group them based on what ads you want to show for the keywords. The more the ad makes sense for the keyword, the more likely someone will click on it; it'll have a higher relevancy. For example, if you're including a type with your keywords, you could break down your list and ad groups that way – an ad group for both "claw hammer" and "ball-peen hammer."

Often people will organize their campaigns similar to how their websites are organized. For a home improvement store, it might look like this:

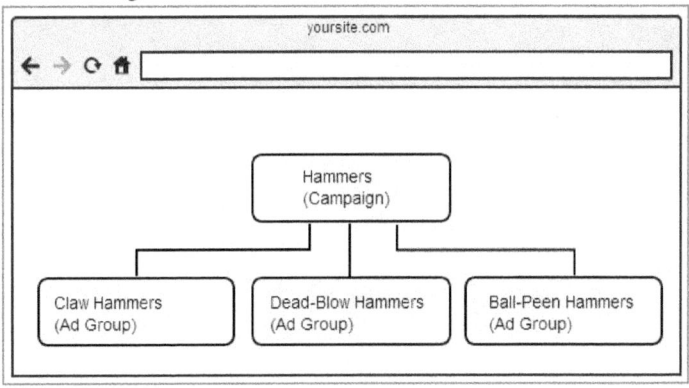

In each ad group, you create ads that display when your keyword is triggered. You can see how you might be able to entice someone to click your ad over other ads that show if you make your text more specific to a particular type of hammer, like claw hammer, than more generic copy. Even if you're attracting just a few more people, this matters more than you might think; you'll see why in a little bit.

Within each ad group, you're allowed to create ads. At a minimum, you should create 3-5 per ad group because it's hard to tell which one will perform the best unless you test different variations. Google will rotate the ads and you'll be able to stop running the ones that don't perform as well as you'd like.

Text ads have character limits because of the amount of space on a page. Below is a list of Google's character limits for ads:

	Max Length (most languages)
Headline:	25 characters
Description line 1:	35 characters
Description line 2:	35 characters
Display URL:	35 characters

Example Ad:
High Quality Claw Hammers
Our sturdy, well made claw hammers
are built to last for 40 years.
www.yoursite.com/claw-hammers

```
Side ad
High Quality Claw Hammers
www.yoursite.com/claw-hammers
Our sturdy, well made claw hammers
are built to last for 40 years.

Top ad
High Quality Claw Hammers
www.yoursite.com/claw-hammers
Our sturdy, well made claw hammers are built to last for 40 years.
```

An ad variation doesn't mean it has to be drastically different. In fact, sometimes it's just a matter of changing one or two words. Who knows which headline will work better: "High Quality Claw Hammers," "Well Built Claw Hammers" or "Long Lasting Claw Hammers?" It's really hard to say without testing which ad is clicked most often.

Make sure that you've read through Google's AdWords guidelines so you know what is permitted and what is forbidden. After you create or change an ad, it will be reviewed by Google to determine if it's allowed. If you violate their policies, they can prevent you from running ads at all which can be a problem if you've come to rely on this method for gaining business.

SEM Strategies

SEM strategies are as varied as the people running the campaigns. Some people will bid below the suggested bids that Google provides and raise the amount if they're not getting enough traffic. Others choose to bid high to ensure that their ads are seen and that they get their initial data back to use for making adjustments as fast as possible.

Some like to start with exact matches and then add more keywords manually over time. Others like to start with broad matches so they get as many related searches as possible, eliminate the ones that don't work and then move to a more restrictive match (exact, phrase, broad match modifier) once they're confident what works.

Some like to run ads on both Google's Search network and Display network (millions of partner sites run by people other than Google). The advantage of appearing on the Display network is that there a better chance to have your ad seen. On the flip side, the people that see your ads on the Display network are typically seeing your ad because it's perceived to be related to the content their reading, not because they're actively looking for your product/service.

There are three things that every good SEM-er does though.

(1) Start With A Smaller Budget And Gradually Increase
Ramp up your budget over time, only after testing. The temptation, especially when you're new, is to start campaigns with the full amount you've budgeted to spend daily. The problem is that you can waste a lot of money that way. Instead, start with a fraction of your budget so you can see

how your ads and keywords perform over at least a couple of weeks.

You want enough data so you know things like:
- How often people are clicking your ads (click-through rate)?
- How much keywords are actually costing per click?
- How often your ads getting seen (number of impressions)?
- Which ads have the highest conversion rates?
- Which keywords have the highest conversion rates?
- Are your cost per conversions still allowing you to be profitable per keyword?

Many businesses try Google AdWords because they get a coupon and they come away frustrated because they blow away their budget without having the chance to make adjustments and optimize their campaign. Not making adjustments and tuning your campaigns is a fast track to failing with SEM, so be cautious in the beginning and then increase your spend.

(2) Be Negative
Negative keywords are a way to prevent traffic from unrelated searches. Add as many negative words as you can think of at the beginning, and continue to do so as you see irrelevant traffic triggering your ads.

To get an idea of some negative keywords, run a search and look through the results to get an idea of what terms might be considered related that you don't want to attract.

When we search for "hammer" on Google, it quickly becomes apparent that there are searches that we show up in when we really don't want to, if we don't add negative keywords. "Nutrition," "museum," "bowling," and "Mac" are not remotely related to what we're selling and will bring the wrong kind of traffic to our ads; they have low relevancy.

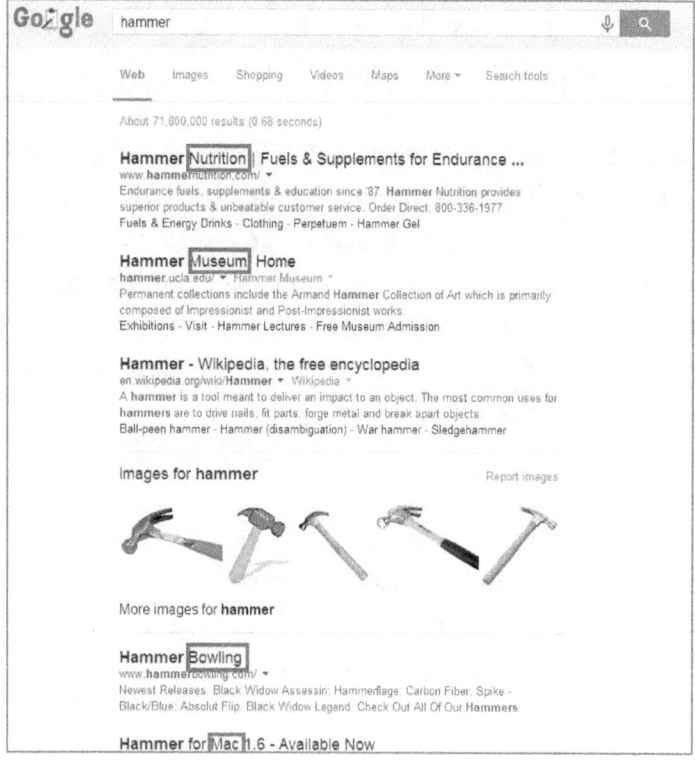

Over time, as you see what searches resulted in clicks, you will see other words that need to be defined as negative keywords to save you money.

(3) Test And Optimize, Repeat
The beauty of having so much control over your ads is that you can make changes any time and have them go into effect immediately (with the exception of new ads). The downside is that since it's so easy, things move fast and the landscape is constantly changing. Competitors will figure out when you're having success and try to steal your traffic while increasing your cost per click. People will get tired of seeing your ads (or may have already clicked on them) and start to ignore them. Aside from that, you should always be trying out new ads to see if you can improve.

So it's pivotal that you **monitor your account regularly, especially at the start of campaigns** when you're still determining what works best. Keep testing ads and keywords and getting rid of the ones that don't work and adding things that might work (that you haven't tried before). Watch trends to see how your cost per click, clickthrough rate and conversion rate move over time. When they deteriorate, you know it's time to test new things and make changes.

Quality Matters

Up to now you might be wondering, what do I care what my clickthrough rate or relevancy is since I don't pay unless someone clicks on my ad? That is true – you don't pay unless someone clicks on your ad. The problem is that Google and Bing make their money from ads, so they don't want to show your ads unless you're going to pay them. At first blush, you might be inclined to think that the amount you bid is what dictates whether your ad is shown, and in what order. In actuality, your bid is only one factor in determining whether your ad is shown.

Google and Bing will assign a **quality score** (1-10) to each of your keywords based on various factors, such as: your clickthrough rate, the quality of your landing page (where you're pointing your ad to) and how relevant your keyword is to your ads. The quality score is calculated each time someone does a search that triggers your ad. It also displays on the keywords tab on your campaign among the data columns.

The gist is that if you have a lower quality score, you're going to have to pay more to have your ad shown. In fact, if your quality score is too low, the search engines may stop showing ads for that keyword altogether.

On the other hand, if you have a high quality score and Google and Bing think that they have a good chance to make money if they show your ad, they're likely to not only show your ad, but move you above others who have a lower tally, even if they are bidding higher.

Quality scores are another thing that you want to check during regular monitoring of your SEM accounts. If you see that your actual cost per click rose or that you're showing up lower in ad positions, your quality score may be to blame.

Who Doesn't Like Free?

OK, it's not exactly free, but Google and Bing frequently offer coupons that let first time advertisers receive a certain amount of credit once try out the marketing service and spend past a specific threshold. Google will often offer a coupon that gives the advertiser a $75 credit once they spend $25.

A lot of times these deals are offered through partners like web hosting companies who have customers that own websites. Sometimes Google will send you one if you've opened an AdWords account but haven't advertised yet. Also, you can sometimes find them by... how else... searching for them.

This chapter covered just the tip of the iceberg for SEM, but it should be enough for you to get started.

15: Resources

SEM Platforms

Bing Keyword Tool (http://www.bing.com/toolbox/keywords) – Use Bing's advertising platform to run ads on Bing and Yahoo. When signing up for an account, do a search for "Bing ad coupons" to see if you can get free ad credits (coupons usually must be applied within a certain amount of days of opening an account).

Google AdWords (http://google.com/AdWords) – Use Google AdWords platform to run ads alongside search results and on partner sites. When signing up for an account, do a search for "AdWords coupons" to see if you can get free ad credits (coupons usually must be applied within a certain amount of days of opening an account).

15: Actionable Checklist

- Have you signed up for Google and Bing ad accounts (they're free)?
- Have you compiled a list of your keywords and your negative keywords?
- Are you running 3-5 ads per ad group?
- How often are you checking your ads?
- Are you stopping keywords and ads that aren't performing well?
- Are your keywords profitable (cost per conversion + other costs still allow a profit)?
- Have you searched for Google and Bing coupons to try out the services?

[16]
Build a Virtual Sales Force

SEO and paid ads are great ways to sell, but they're far from the only way. One thing you should consider is creating a **virtual sales force – people who sell on the Internet on your behalf.** It sounds expensive, but it's actually very affordable considering that you only pay them after you're paid. Some may think that this sounds like a pipedream, but it's actually a very common practice across the Internet.

There are many reasons why you should consider making other people part of your web selling strategy.

Who Do You Affiliate With?

Affiliate programs are ways websites and blog owners, also referred to as publishers, can make money when they refer sales to a business.

One of the biggest, if not the biggest, affiliate programs is run by Amazon.com and is called **Amazon Associates**. Publishers apply to participate in Amazon Associates, and if they're approved, they get paid on every sale they refer to the e-commerce giant. To refer someone means that a visitor on the referring website clicked a link to Amazon's site (or a particular product) that contains code to indicate who referred the person.

Most of the time people aren't aware that a link is an affiliate one. In fact, it's very likely that you've clicked on affiliate links before. One place that affiliate links are extremely popular are sites where people write product reviews. For example, if you do a search on "[product name] reviews," there are likely to be sites that pop-up where someone is writing reviews.

When we do a search of "accounting software reviews" and click one of the review sites, we see this on their site – a "Visit Site" link:

Total Score	★★★★★	★★★★★
Price	$12.95/month+	$183.96
Details	Read Review	Read Review
Website	Visit Site	Visit Site

When you click on the link, you can immediately tell that it's an affiliate link because of the URL. It contains "affisignup" and also has a bunch of variables near the end (indicated by the "?") that are used to identify the referrer.

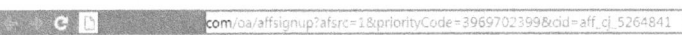

Sometimes, the affiliates will "mask" their details so you won't see the variables, so this isn't a sure fire way to tell. Also, variables can be used for other purposes on a Website. However, in this case it was obvious that it is not only an affiliate, but one from Commission Junction ("cj" in the URL).

Affiliate programs are used across all kinds of industries and presented on all types of sites. Here are just a few examples:

- Business Opportunities – Sites that talk about ways to earn money
- E-Commerce – Product reviews or news and sites that list deals (coupon sites)
- Education/Training – Sites that provide information about college prep, trades or schools

- Financial Services – Sites that talk about credit cards
- Health/Fitness – Sites that mention fitness or dietary products
- Software – Software review or white paper sites
- Travel – Sites that have links to book with airlines, hotels, or cars

How Do Affiliate Programs Work?

With affiliate programs, participants are paid a commission, usually a percentage of the amount of a sale that is set by you, the program owner. This commission amount can be simple or complex. Commission can be set up so all sales for all affiliates result in the same amount, 10% per sale. Or different products can result in different commissions (like Amazon does). There can be a tiered structure where high performing affiliates earn a larger amount than regular ones.

An affiliate program can also pay out per lead. For example, an affiliate receives $3 every time they refer someone who fills out a form on a landing page.

Acceptance into an affiliate program can be based on an application and manual approvals or it can be automatic. If you're creating an affiliate program of your own, you set-up the terms or the affiliate program, indicate what they can and can't do. A common rule is that affiliates can't bid on your brand name through SEM because this would pit them against you and raise the cost per click bids.

The terms of an affiliate program will explain when an affiliate will get paid. Affiliates don't get paid right away. First of all, there has to be some time to make sure that the sale stands, that there's no return/refund or fraud. Otherwise the program loses money to the affiliate. A timetable is set in the terms that says when payments are made, generally monthly or quarterly. Most programs also have a threshold that needs to be earned before a payment is made. It doesn't really make sense to pay an affiliate $2.51 after the transaction costs (for both sites). A typical minimum payout for affiliates is $50-$100.

Besides the obligation to pay as outlined in the terms, there are other things that can be done to help make sales easier. While you can allow affiliates to refer people to you through simple text links, you can also provide them other options. Create banner ads as a way for them to visually attract clicks to your site. You can also create sales, promotions or coupon codes that affiliates can mention to their readers to entice them to visit your site.

It's your affiliate program so you can set the parameters and terms. Just make sure you're providing the tools to help make their job of selling your product or program as easy and attractive as possible.

Affiliate Software

There's no shortage of affiliate program management software out there. The majority are hosted on the Internet and you pay a monthly fee.

At the bare minimum, affiliate software should:
- Allow people to apply to be affiliates
- Allow for manual or automatic approval of applicants (depending on preference)
- Keep track of affiliates
- Keep track of how much affiliates have earned in commission
- Allow affiliates to log in and see reporting on the sales they've referred and their earnings
- Allow you to remove users who violate the terms
- Provide reporting on how much is money owed to affiliates, how many people are signing up and how much you've earned in sales from your program

Depending on the software, there are many more sophisticated features offered. One useful one that you may need, depending on the volume of sales you receive, is the ability to make payments directly through the software. Some affiliate software allows you to make payments after integrating with your bank account and tracks when the money was sent. In fact, some can be scheduled to make the payments for you when an affiliate has exceeded their minimum payment threshold.

How Do I Get Affiliates?

To begin getting affiliates organically, start by telling your current customers and fans about your affiliate program. Since they already believe in you and your products/services, they make great advocates who are more than willing to tell others to check out your site. Also, make sure that you have a page or section of your website that describes how the program works and have a link to it in the footer so visitors will see it.

Network

If you want to accelerate the growth of your affiliate program or you feel like you're ready to take the next step from organic growth, join an **affiliate network**.

Affiliate networks match programs with publishers. Publishers apply to be in the network and if they're approved, they can see the listing of all of the affiliate programs and can apply to participate. Depending on the network, thousands of affiliate programs are listed (segmented by industry).

This can get pricey depending on the network, but it can also be well worth it. Think about having exposure to tens to hundreds of thousands of publishers who are interested in affiliate programs and know how to refer business. Aside from allowing people to see your program in the listings, you can also contact publishers if you're a part of the network.

16: Resources

Create Banners

BannerFlow (http://bannerflow.com) – Software that you can use to create banners where you pay by the month. They offer a free trial to test the software.

BannerSnack (http://bannersnack.com) – Software to create your own banners. BannerSnack allows you to create banners for free that contain a watermark. If you want to remove the watermark, pay for a month of their Pro plan and download your banner.

Affiliate Networks

These are just a few of the options when looking at places to market your affiliate program and recruit publishers.

Click Bank (http://clickbank.com)

Click Booth (http://clickbooth.com)

Commission Junction (http://cj.com)

Linkshare (http://linkshare.com)

ShareASale (http://shareasale.com)

16: Actionable Checklist

- Have you thought about establishing an affiliate program for your business?
- What types of things could you include in your affiliate program?
- Is it worth the cost of the program to increase the amount of websites driving traffic to yours?
- Do you have a group of people who own websites or blogs (publishers) that would be interested in helping sell your products/services?
- How much could you afford to pay in commission (as a percent of sale or per lead)?

[17]
The After Party

Attracting a visitor to your site and making a sale shouldn't be your end goal.

Aim for creating repeat customers.

After all, it's well documented that luring back customers is much cheaper than obtaining new ones. Previous customers know what you offer and why they should buy from you (i.e. your level of service, quality of product, etc.). With new prospects, you have to educate them on what you offer, why they need it and why they should buy from you.

If High Returns On Investment (ROI) Interest You...

Even though it's not as flashy or "cutting edge" as other digital tools, email is still the form of marketing with the highest ROI. While you can send direct mail to people, it's still hard to beat the ROI on email since you don't have to pay for postage, a list or materials for each person you're trying to reach.

To get people on your list, you need them to opt-in; they have to give your permission to add them to your email lists. The way to do this is through a very simple form, located somewhere prominent on your site (like at the very top) – or even in a separate pop-up window that someone sees before going anywhere else on your site.

Don't make people hunt for your opt-in box – if they have to look for it, they won't give you their information.

Make sure that sign-up boxes for your email list are obvious and stand out. While it annoys some visitors, a lot of websites now have pop-up boxes that appear when you're visiting a page, so they're immediately shown the offer to join their email list (often graying out the rest of the site).

Here's one that immediately displayed on Pottery Barn's website:

Make Money on the Internet | 319

Similarly, Gap.com shows this on entry:

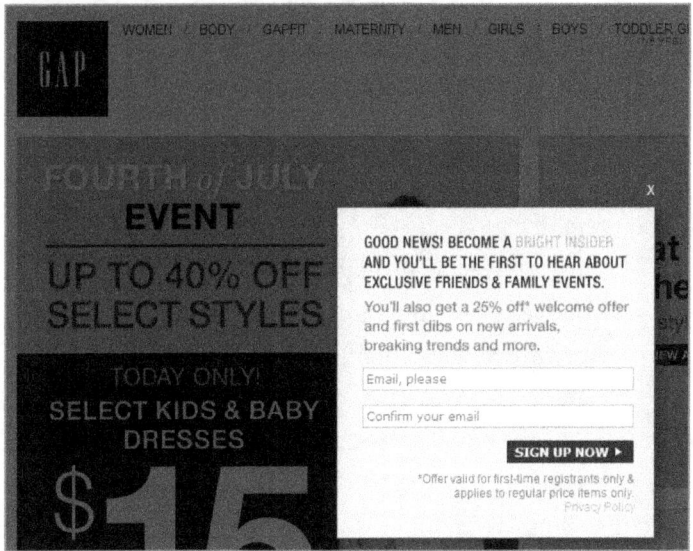

There's also another approach of having a sign-up box in the footer of pages, like Barnes and Noble and Zappos.

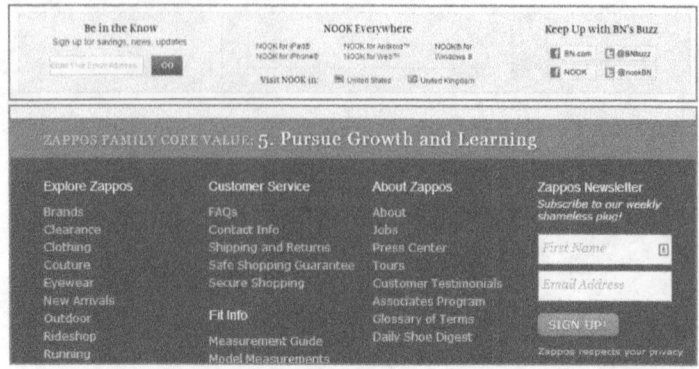

Email Made Easy

While **email marketing** may not be sexy, it is established, so there are plenty of good, affordable tools out there. At a minimum, you should look for email software that provides:

- Professional templates (for email designs)
- Code for your site so people can sign-up for your email list
- Ease of use (i.e. formatting, adding content, etc.)
- Analytics (i.e. tracking how many read, open and forwarded your email)

Almost all of the email software sites offer free trials so you can see how easy it is to use and review what templates are available. Some companies, such as MailChimp, offer a free plan that gives you access to most of their features, but not all (you upgrade to a paid subscription for some things).

To entice visitors to your site to join your mailing list, offer something that they want. Don't leave the offer generic with, "Join Our Mailing List." Sure a few people may sign-up, but you're sure to miss out on new subscribers. With such a generic offer, you're not indicating what the benefit of joining the list is.

Ten years ago that may have worked. Now, most sites have at least one email list and you're competing against them. You have to convince the person that what they get from you won't be spam and they'll find it valuable to them.

As we mentioned earlier, you could use a lead incentive, offer something that the person gets for free when they subscribe. If you want to entice people to join your list without a lead incentive, then give specific benefits. Maybe that's offering them "exclusive" coupons/deals via email, be the first to receive news, get free tips/tutorials, or invitations to special events. Be creative and make it worthwhile for them. In return, people will opt-in to your email list and remain subscribers that actually open your emails.

Remarketing/Retargeting

You may not know the terms **remarketing or retargeting,** but you've likely experienced it before. Retargeting, or remarketing if you use Google's terminology, is when you visit a website once, and after you leave the site, you start to see ads for that site.

The ads "follow" you around the Internet.

Retargeting ads tend to convert well relative to other types of ads because you're bringing back people that already have visited your site. That means they have some familiarity with what you're offering, and if they click on your ad and are willing to visit again, it can greatly increase your chance of making a sale.

If you want to see an example, try visiting AdRoll or Perfect Audience's site and then going to Facebook. Soon you'll see ads retargeting you. Here's an example of Perfect Audience using retargeting:

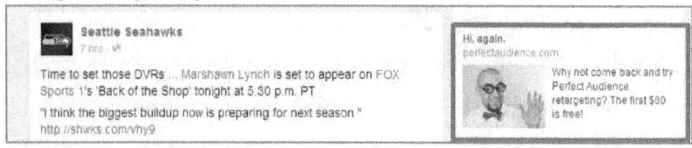

You can even take it down to the product level. Amazon, Zappos and Home Depot often do retargeting and if you visit a product on their page, there's a good chance that you'll see an ad for that very same product show up on other sites.

How Does Retargeting Work?

Retargeting works by placing a snippet of code (a cookie) on your site that will track if someone visited your site. The code is supplied by whatever service you are using for retargeting. If you use Google, then your ad will show on websites in their network. Their vast network includes sites where publishers participate in Google's AdSense program and receive a portion of the revenue for showing ads.

Aside from Google, there are third parties like Perfect Audience and AdRoll that don't have their own ad network but leverage others. This lets them place your ads across not only Google's network, but also on Facebook, Yahoo, Microsoft, and Twitter. They charge based on a cost per impression (CPM) basis, where you pay for every thousand times your ad appears, regardless of whether it was clicked or not. These third parties make money by taking a portion of the CPM amount.

At a bare minimum, test retargeting to see if it works for you, even if you're skeptical. You can set a small budget and see what your ROI is. If the ads are profitable, increase your spend until they aren't. Aside from recouping potentially lost sales from visitors who didn't buy, it will bring back people who did make purchases from you as return customers.

Don't expect people to come back if they didn't buy from just because they visited your site. It typically takes people at least three exposures to your name before they can remember a brand or offering.

Make it easy for them to think of you by retargeting and you'll be rewarded with sales.

17: Resources

Retargeting/Remarketing

AdRoll (http://adroll.com) – This is a service that lets you to retarget across different networks and social media. They offer a free trial to determine if it will work for you. You pay on a cost per impression (CPM) basis, which means you pay for every thousand people that see your ad (regardless of if they click on your ad or not) and AdRoll takes a portion of that amount as their fee.

Google Remarketing (http://www.google.com/ads/innovations/remarketing.html) – Google remarketing shows ads to people that have visited your site before. Their ads are limited to sites showing Google ads (which is millions), but you could pay less for your ads because there's no third party service provider involved (who you have to pay).

Perfect Audience (http://perfectaudience.com) – Similar to AdRoll, Perfect Audience lets you retarget across different networks and offers a free trial. They make their money by taking a portion of the amount you're paying to show your ads (on a CPM basis).

17: Actionable Checklist

- How are you building your email list(s)?
- What other ways can you attract people to your mailing list?
- Can you improve your offer to people joining your mailing list?
- Have you tried retargeting?

[18]

What's Next? Start Selling!

Ok, so there you go. By the time you get to this point, we have carefully examined the components that come together to form a successful web selling machine. You have just about everything you need to start turning your website into profits.

We've given you the tools and ideas to get you off the ground. In fact, we've given you so many that you're probably going to want to just start with a few if you're brand new to this. If you're more experienced and are having some success, take some of the concepts and integrate them with what you're already doing.

We didn't deep dive into everything but wanted to give you an overview so you understand your options, have the resources and can start today.

No matter what we tell you, you won't know what works for you specifically until you take action. Your business is unique – your offering is unique – so your sales and advertising strategy will be unique.

The worst thing you can do is sit back and think. And wait. And read. And research. And plan.

Why?

Because when you're spending all your time doing that, you're not making any moves to build your list or drive sales.

Of course you have to take the time to map out a strategy and establish a budget, but once that's in place... do something.

If you're interested in learning additional marketing tips and news for free, visit our website blog (http://thinkstrategy.com/blog)

MEET YOUR AUTHORS

RYAN CHIN

Ryan is the co-founder of Think Strategy (http://thinkstrategy.com), a full-service digital marketing agency. He brings over a decade of marketing and technology experience to his clients. Working as a Management Consultant at Accenture, he delivered solutions to complex problems for Fortune 500 companies. After leaving Accenture, he started an e-commerce business and became an eBay Top Rated Seller and one of Amazon.com's Top 25% sellers. Prior to joining Think Strategy, he founded two startups.

He graduated from the University of Washington with an undergraduate degree in Business and holds an MBA from Seattle University.

Ryan's previous publications include The Beginner's Guide to Building a Successful eBay Business, a book that teaches people how to excel on the e-commerce site.

ANGIE SALISBURY

Angie is the owner of Annibury, LLC, an expert business writer and sought-after communication strategist and ghostwriter with nearly 20 years of experience. Having worked with companies ranging from small, independently owned companies to multi-billion dollar, international corporations, Angie works with clients in a wide-range of industries to help them develop the perfect communication plan. She is able to take any concept or idea and bring it to life.

Angie graduated from Bowling Green State University before going on to Florida Atlantic University for her MA. While working on her PhD at Kent State University, Angie decided to make the leap into the business world and never looked back. When not writing and copyediting, Angie is spending time with her dogs, at the gym or working on her latest grand needlework project.

Angie is also a life coach and is currently working on two soon-to-be-released books.

www.ingramcontent.com/pod-product-compliance
Lightning Source LLC
Chambersburg PA
CBHW051759170526
45167CB00005B/1805